2021

The State of Religion & Young People
NAVIGATING UNCERTAINTY

Springtide™
RESEARCH INSTITUTE

A note about the cover:

The cover illustrates the feeling of "spiraling" we often colloquially associate with experiences of uncertainty or doubt in life. But for young people, these uncertainties—these spirals—do not indicate doom or dread; they are, like our cover, just the backdrop to daily life. In addition to a symbol of uncertainty, we were inspired by the way spirals represent a kind of unbounded circle. A spiral moves away from its initial, closed form as a circle and toward a freer structure, one that nonetheless takes inspiration from that original shape. It echoes the way young people increasingly resist closed systems of meaning for something more free-flowing and organic. In short, the spiral reminds us of what we call "Faith Unbundled," a new way of thinking about this generation's approach to faith that includes making space for variation, personalization, and uncertainty as they journey through their lives.

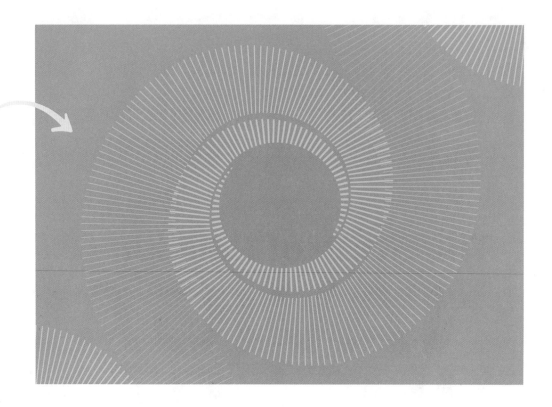

All the resources referenced in numbered marginal notes throughout this report are compiled in a list both at the end of this book and at *springtideresearch.org/the-state-2021-resources*. These resources include podcasts and blog posts from young people, as well as conversations Springtide is having with outside experts, deep dives with Dr. Josh Packard, and more.

Springtide
RESEARCH INSTITUTE

Mission

Compelled by the urgent desire to listen and attend to the lives of young people (ages 13 to 25), Springtide Research Institute is committed to understanding the distinct ways new generations experience and express community, identity, and meaning.

We exist at the intersection of religious and human experience in the lives of young people. And we're here to listen.

We combine quantitative and qualitative research to reflect and amplify the lived realities of young people as they navigate shifting social, cultural, and religious landscapes. Delivering fresh data and actionable insights, we equip those who care about young people to care better.

A Springtide Tribute.
A Promise. A Pledge.

 TO YOU

. . . who are young, full of wonder and possibility. You who are navigating some of life's most important questions and most tumultuous waters. You who are sometimes flourishing and sometimes floundering and oftentimes both. You who are at once being and becoming.

We dedicate our work to your thriving.

We dedicate ourselves to understanding your inner and outer lives.

 TO YOU

. . . who are fiercely devoted to young people. You who advocate for and walk alongside young people with steadiness. You who are unwavering amid the waves.

We offer our research as an aid to the role you already play.

We offer ourselves as allies in accompaniment.

AND TO

. . . the waves that crash, the currents that bend and beckon, the dark depths, and the effervescent crests. To this all-important period of life: worthy of considered listening and faithful retelling, worthy of companionship, worthy of care.

We situate our work at this intersection of human and religious experience in the lives of young people: a space of ebb and flow, of calm and chaos, of clear and murky moments.

A space we are dedicated to exploring and engaging

WITH YOU.

SAP Dedication

Watch how members of our Springtide Ambassadors Program bring our Springtide Tribute to life with their creative interpretation and filmmaking skills.

springtideresearch.org/the-state-2021-resources

Contents

Part I: Navigating Uncertainty

Part II: Faith Unbundled

Conclusion

> **Unbundling is the name of the spiritual game, at least for the foreseeable future. Springtide helps us understand what that means, and how to serve young people in the midst of it.**
>
> —Casper ter Kuile

Foreword

By the time I attended my third wedding that summer, about a decade ago, the trend was clear. Instead of having religious ceremonies led by ordained ministers in churches, my friends were coming up with more personalized marriage rituals, inviting peers to officiate in beautiful outdoor settings. Often these ceremonies wove together secular sources—poetry, music, family stories—with religious ones: Bible readings, a breaking of the glass, a blessing. Most of these friends might describe themselves as religiously "nothing in particular," though a couple might have said "just Christian." But all of them felt a hunger for something spiritual in their lives, including a way to mark the spiritual significance of their wedding day, even while they were uneasy with traditional, institutional ways of doing so.

Springtide's new report *The State of Religion & Young People 2021: Navigating Uncertainty* is brimming with insight about the way young people (ages 13 to 25) are figuring out how to draw on religious and spiritual support to make it through life's challenges and to celebrate its joys, and the ways they are increasingly doing so outside of formal structures of faith. At the heart of the report is the notion of unbundling. Rather than finding one's religious identity, practice, community, and language in one consistent source, more and more young people are piecing together their inner life by drawing on various traditions, familial lineages, and wisdom sources.

Is this evidence of a kind of selfish spiritual path among young people? An approach to questions of faith that smacks of consumerism, with a marketplace of religious commodities, all up for grabs, and little concern for questions of appropriation or context? No, argues this report.

Rather than trying to extract the elements of faith from different religious contexts (which sociologists of religion might recognize as Robert Bellah's *Sheilaism*), young people are trying to integrate their existing multiplicities. By finding ways to piece together their varying family histories, geographic and cultural contexts, personal interests and sensibilities, young people are attempting to experience a wholeness and connection that demands curiosity and flexibility if they are to stay true to the people they understand themselves to be.

It's no surprise that young people resist a fixed definition about what it means to be religious today. Just as gender expressions, sexualities, and racial identities are now understood on a richer spectrum and grounded in intersectionality, young Americans are reimagining religiosity, spirituality, or faith as something that opposes a stark "in" or "out," "this" or "that" way of compartmentalizing. Indeed, in my experience—both professionally as someone watching these trends, and personally as I witness my peers marking life's biggest moments by forging new territory between and among various traditions—I continue to see that young people find institutional identity or whole group cohesion not only unattractive but often untrustworthy.

Unbundling is the name of the spiritual game, at least for the foreseeable future. Springtide helps us understand what that means, and how to serve young people in the midst of it.

Casper ter Kuile

Casper ter Kuile is the author of The Power of Ritual, *the cofounder of Sacred Design Lab, and cocreator of hit podcast "Harry Potter and the Sacred Text." He served as a Ministry Innovation Fellow at Harvard Divinity School between 2016 and 2021 after graduating with master's degrees in public policy and divinity. Learn more about his work at* www.caspertk.com *and on Twitter @caspertk.*

From Springtide's Executive Director

In the 2020 article "Science Explains Why Uncertainty Is So Hard on Our Brains," Markham Heid discusses the science behind uncertainty, explaining that it is at the source of anxiety disorders and panic attacks and may even be the basis of fear. Heid interviews psychologist Jack Nitschke who puts it plainly: "Uncertainty lays the groundwork for anxiety because anxiety is always future-oriented."

Uncertainty and change are hallmarks of being young—so much lies ahead, so many decisions are faced for the first time—but this past year has brought unprecedented challenges. Uncertainty has been the air we breathe. For young people, the already-uncertain aspects of life have been amplified. Heid notes that "uncertainty acts like rocket fuel for worry; it causes people to see threats everywhere they look, and . . . it makes them more likely to react emotionally in response to those threats."

At Springtide, we listen to young people, ages 13 to 25, and amplify their voices through quantitative and qualitative sociological research. This year we knew we had to focus on uncertainty, including the role it plays in faith and the ways and extent to which young people dealing with uncertainty or difficulty turn to faith or religion. They have been searching, and sometimes finding, ways that spirituality, religious practice, and belief can help them deal with uncertainty and anxiety. So who are they turning to for those solutions?

Spoiler alert: They aren't turning to religion, at least not in the traditional sense. But the majority of young people nonetheless tell us they are religious. And our data suggest good news: Religious young people are faring better than the non religious in all aspects of their well-being, including when navigating uncertainty.

And although the majority of young people Springtide surveyed consider themselves at least slightly religious (71%) or spiritual (78%), the majority aren't turning to religious institutions in times of difficulty. This is despite the fact that these institutions across the board have rituals, beliefs, practices, and communities that aim, in part, to help humans cope with uncertainty.

Why, at this highly uncertain time in history, are young people bypassing religious institutions for other ways of coping amid uncertainty? What is the reason for this disconnect, what can be done to bridge that divide, and how might communities (religious or not) adapt and grow to better serve the needs of today's young people?

Young people are increasingly less likely to be engaged with institutional forms of religious expression. Decades-long trends continue: for a large and growing segment of young people, religiosity is increasingly decoupled from institutions, even as they express high levels of religious belief, practice, and identity. These personal, social, and religious reasons start to explain *why* there's a disconnect between young people and institutions. But the cost of this disconnect remains the same no matter the reason: young people tell us institutional responses aren't meeting their needs.

Faith Unbundled, a concept we explore in this report, describes the way young people are constructing the elements of faith by turning to many religious and non religious sources. We asked expert practitioners—religious, secular, and spiritual—committed to the flourishing of young people to weigh in on best practices for supporting this emerging, unbundled path of religious exploration. They offer us a vision of care that is at once adaptable to the needs of young people, while still drawing from the deep well of their own traditions.

The State of Religion & Young People 2021: Navigating Uncertainty explores reasons for the disconnect between young people and religious institutions in times of uncertainty. A lot has shifted in the religious, cultural, and social landscape. We have studied the landscape, listened closely to the experiences of young people, and integrated the perspectives of practitioners.

One thing is abundantly clear. This youngest generation, Gen Z, is pressing forward, exploring the boundaries of their faith, constructing meaning, navigating uncertainty, and encountering the divine in new ways. The only question that remains is whether you'll be there to guide them.

Josh Packard, PhD

As you read, connect with us @WeAreSpringtide on Facebook, Instagram, or Twitter and use #religionandyoung people2021 to join the conversation. Sign up for our e-newsletter at *springtideresearch.org*, or send us an email to let us know how you're helping young people navigate uncertainty.

Introduction

Welcome to *The State of Religion & Young People 2021: Navigating Uncertainty*.

This is Springtide's flagship report, one that annually explores the religious lives of young people ages 13 to 25. The 2021 report is the product of a full year of research, over 10,000 surveys featuring questions about young people's beliefs, practices, behaviors, relationships, and this year's focus: ways young people are navigating uncertainty. In addition to surveying, we conducted qualitative interviews with young people along the same themes, listening for the nuance that emerges only through conversation.

Our passion for listening to young people extends beyond quantitative and qualitative research. We invite more young people to participate in our work and weigh in on our research. Our Springtide Ambassadors Program brings a cohort of young people together with the Springtide team to discuss their lived experience in light of reports, to formulate research questions, to interpret and discuss data, and to provide insight, often in unforeseen ways, through wide-ranging conversations.

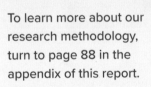

To learn more about our research methodology, turn to page 88 in the appendix of this report.

We release a season of our *Voices of Young People Podcast* to augment each report with reflections from young people. Finally, Springtide interns, who serve in many areas—research, publicity, publishing, and community engagement—help us assess our work as an institute, and they contribute their own insights and wisdom to this endeavor. This combination of data and lived experiences enriches everything you read from Springtide.

Last year we published the first of these reports, *The State of Religion & Young People 2020: Relational Authority*. In that report, we introduced the concept of Relational Authority: a framework for building bonds of trust amid new cultural, social, and religious realities. We recognize the continued importance of this framework, especially the need for adults in the lives of young people to practice integrity, transparency, listening, care, and expertise in a year in which so many young people expressed broken trust, political polarization, a sense of isolation, and more. This 2021 report builds on that framework.

> **Learn more about Relational Authority by downloading the free report**
> *springtideresearch.org/the-state-2020*

After the turmoil and tensions brought on by the COVID-19 pandemic, the murder of George Floyd and the global protests that followed, and the lead-up and aftermath of the 2020 US presidential election (to name a few issues), Springtide knew there was a need for a better understanding about how young people navigate and cope with uncertainty, and how trusted adults can support young people during times of uncertainty, whether that uncertainty is brief or long-term. Note that we say it's the trusted adults' role to *support*: not fix, not solve, not force certainty where uncertainty arises.

We'll highlight Springtide resources throughout this report, the kind that young people create and contribute to in podcasts and blog posts, as well as conversations we're having with outside experts, deep dives with Dr. Josh Packard, and more. All the resources referenced in numbered marginal notes throughout this report are compiled in a list both at the end of this book and at *springtideresearch.org /the-state-2021-resources*.

Over and over in our surveys, interviews, and even in our reading and conversations within the wider social sciences, we see that young people aren't looking for quick fixes to complex issues. They don't necessarily expect immediate resolution or certainty. Colette, a young mother, told Springtide how she responds to overwhelming, difficult, or uncertain experiences:

> I like to shut everything off for a moment. So I'll either meditate, I'll do yoga, I'll listen to music, like self-care, maybe take a bath, or just go on a walk, anything to stop thinking about whatever stressed me out. I know that doesn't fix the problem, but it does help momentarily.
>
> —Colette, 23

Like Colette, many young people don't feel the need to "fix the problem" immediately. Sometimes they just need to bear the problem, breathe deeply, or take a walk during a difficult time. A little over half (51%) of all young people ages 13 to 25 tell us, "I am comfortable with not having all the answers." Sometimes they are just trying to endure the uncertainty if it's not possible to escape or resolve it right away; often it's not. And for many young people, this insight is the first clue about *why* they don't turn to religion when navigating uncertain or difficult times:

2

Watch Dr. Josh Packard and Ryan Burge discuss the "nones" of religion, and young people who are growing into religion.

springtideresearch.org /the-state-2021-resources

58% of young people ages 13 to 25 told us, **"I do not like to be told answers about faith and religion, I'd rather discover my own answers."**

54% report, **"Religious communities try to fix my problem, instead of just being there for me."**

They aren't looking for a solution to uncertainty, which is not only a fact of life but also a fact of adolescence and young adulthood, as well as a vivid fact of our current cultural moment. Young people are looking for relationships built on presence and listening, not advice and fixing. More than half of young people (51%) told us that the most useful or important thing a person did to help them during uncertainty was to "just let [them] talk." Ally, a high school senior, has several adults she can talk to. At the heart of these relationships is "wholehearted trust":

> I talked to my mom about it. I talked to my therapist. I talked to my college counselor and some advisors at my school that I trust wholeheartedly. I just, I try to talk to people who I know have the best interest for me when it comes to, like, my future, because sometimes making decisions by yourself is hard. With these kinds of decisions, no one can make them for me, but I like having feedback from others who care.
>
> —Ally, 17

Instead of people who make the decision for them, young people look for people with whom they can discuss big decisions and feel empowered to make the right one. Instead of solutions, they look for relationships with people who will see them through to the other side of uncertainty, whatever that other side looks like.

Religious leaders often already know what this kind of presence amid uncertainty can and does look like: think of the ministry of accompaniment in the Christian tradition, the work of Muslim chaplains in hospital, university, or military settings, or the Jewish practice of sitting shiva with the bereaved. These types of rituals or practices are embedded deep within all kinds of traditions, whether religious or even humanist. Often they just need to be accessed and offered in new ways.

To be effective, those trusted guides will do well to understand and honor the new ways Gen Z is navigating questions of uncertainty, specifically the way many young people's religious seeking is unbundled.

A CLOSER LOOK

In this report, you'll find three special features, called "A Closer Look," that dive deeper into young people's experience of the COVID-19 pandemic, the disconnect between religious institutions and young people, and some thinkers' engagement with the concept of an "unbundled" faith.

Watch Dr. Josh Packard explain why a sociological approach is needed to navigate religious identity among young people.

springtideresearch.org /the-state-2021-resources

In Part I of *The State of Religion & Young People 2021,* we explore the disconnect between young people and religious institutions, even amid times of uncertainty. This means investigating the experience of uncertainty *and* the ways young people are already responding to those experiences, whether those responses are religious, relational, or something else entirely. In order to better understand this disconnect, we look at the reasons young people report not turning to religious institutions during difficult times, and also examples of the times they do depend on their religious faith, communities, identity, or practices. **A portrait emerges of a new type of faith, one that is not bound to one tradition or institution or community but is unbundled.**

In Part II, we explore Faith Unbundled: what it is, how it relates to uncertainty, and why it matters for religious leaders today. *Curiosity, wholeness, connection,* and *flexibility* are the hallmarks of Faith Unbundled—that is, they are the qualities that guide how young people are pursuing and discerning religious questions. In addition to listening to the voices of young people through surveys and interviews, we listened to religious and secular practitioners and experts who weighed in on the unbundled quality of young people's faith today.

Part II presents reflections from four experts who witness Faith Unbundled in their own contexts:

Rev. Sumi Loundon Kim
Buddhist Chaplain at Yale University

Chris Stedman
Director of the Humanist Center of Minnesota and professor of religion

Nima Dahir
Cofounder of Refuge, an organization mentoring young adult refugees and a PhD candidate at Stanford studying belonging and community among immigrants

Rabbi Joshua Stanton
Rabbi at East End Temple in Manhattan and a Senior Fellow at CLAL

Each offers insights rooted in expertise and experience about how best to serve young people in light of this emerging spirituality.

Season 5: *The Voices of Young People Podcast*

Season 5 of *The Voices of Young People Podcast* features ten young people telling us, in their own words, about their experiences of faith, doubt, and uncertainty. Listen to the episodes at *springtideresearch.org/podcast*.

Abby, 24, Michigan   **Amethyst, 23, Illinois**   **Christian, 22, Pennsylvania**   **Daniel, 22, North Carolina**   **Elyse, 15, Massachusetts**

Josué, 25, California   **Lily, 15, Minnesota**   **Lucy, 21, Pennsylvania**   **Saad, 26, Illinois**   **Zaina, 16, Massachusetts**

In this season, we invited young people to tell us what "faith" means to them, including why or whether they would use that term to describe their inner life. We asked where they feel most connected to their center of meaning, why and how they've come to identify with this faith or set of values, and the ways they've relied on it as they navigate life's joys, difficulties, and uncertainties.

The Voices of Young People
PODCAST

PART I

NAVIGATING UNCERTAINTY

Facing Life's Biggest Questions

Young people are facing some of life's biggest questions: Who am I? What should I do with my life? What commitments do I want to make now that could alter the course of my life: commitments to another person, a school program, a career path, a new city? Young people deal daily with questions about how and who to be, where and to what to belong, how and whether to believe—in Sikhism or socialism, Tik Tok influencers or media talking heads. They are perpetually navigating major decisions, and with each decision they are building the persons they will become. But even once a young person begins to feel settled about who they are or what they believe, they feel additional pressure about whether to show that to the world. Elsa, a young Hindu woman in her senior year of high school, offers an enlightening observation:

> Everyone is just trying to live their lives to show a certain face out to the world, not who they truly are or their personality. They can be battling a million different things and nobody will know, and they don't want to show anyone because they want to keep a certain persona up to the entire world.

—Elsa, 18

Many of these major questions have uncertainty at their heart. Indeed, adolescence and young adulthood are marked by transitions and changes, a perpetual state of not knowing what's next. This uncertainty was even more pronounced in the past year. As we wrote in *The New Normal: 8 Ways to Care for Gen Z in a Post-Pandemic World*, "For young people between the ages of 13 and 25, it's not uncommon for every year to be different from the next. There's no 'normal' to return to. [In 2020,] their world turned upside down just as they were starting to find their footing."

Elsa, the young woman quoted on the previous page, wonders if faith anchors other young people who might feel lost when navigating such major questions or feeling pressure to keep up a persona:

> I feel like having a faith or having something that can ground them to earth and to the very ground that they're standing on can help them get through a lot of things. And if they really believe that doing something with their faith works, maybe it can help them get through a lot of dark times.
>
> —Elsa, 18

But our data show that even though the majority of young people identify as religious (71%) or spiritual (78%), most aren't turning to religion—whether religious communities, leaders, practices, or beliefs—to help guide them in moments of uncertainty. This is true even of the young people who tell us they attend, believe in, or identify with a particular religious tradition. Of the young people who identified as "very religious," less than half (40%) told us they found connecting with their faith community helpful during challenging or uncertain times; only 23% of those who consider themselves moderately religious found this helpful. Only 1 in 5 young people in general agree with the statement "I use faith as a guide when I am confused about things."

4

Watch some of Springtide's ambassadors discuss returning to campus in the fall and what the pandemic has meant for them.

springtideresearch.org /the-state-2021-resources

71%
of young people say they are religious.

78%
of young people say they are spiritual.

Of the young people who identified as "very religious," **less than half (40%)** told us they found connecting with their faith community helpful during challenging or uncertain times.

By and large, young people aren't turning to religious institutions, practices, services, or leaders in times of uncertainty. And whether or not religious leaders are *trying* to reach young people, our data show that they aren't reaching them. When we asked young people about their experience one year into the pandemic, only 10% of young people ages 13 to 25 told us that a faith leader reached out to them personally during the year.

If anyone outside of your home has reached out to you personally, who was it?

Participants were allowed to select more than one option.

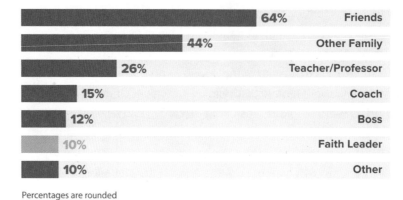

64%	Friends
44%	Other Family
26%	Teacher/Professor
15%	Coach
12%	Boss
10%	Faith Leader
10%	Other

Percentages are rounded

Only 10% *of young people ages 13 to 25 told us that a faith leader reached out to them personally during the pandemic.*

Our data show a clear disconnect between young people and religious institutions. But even with this disconnect, our data don't reveal a loss of interest in spiritual and religious questions among young people, or even a loss of faith.

Religious traditions have long-established ways of dealing with uncertainty and upheaval. Perhaps more than any other modern institution, religion is unafraid of life's biggest questions; indeed, many religious traditions, rituals, beliefs, and practices face these questions head on. Faith is, in a sense, a way of responding to the experience of not knowing what comes next, in both big and small matters. And yet, young people (even those who identify as religious or spiritual) are *not* turning to those traditions and rituals during personal times of uncertainty.

Watch Dr. Josh Packard and Derrick Scott III talk about how non-white and queer young people are navigating church.

*springtideresearch.org
/the-state-2021-resources*

In *The State of Religion & Young People 2020*, we reported that programs alone—even highly engaging and well-attended programs—are not enough to give young people a sense of trust or belonging within an organization. Young people need trusted mentors who practice listening, integrity, transparency, care, and expertise. Our *New Normal* guide makes it clear that young people dealing with adolescence and young adulthood amid an unprecedented pandemic didn't turn to religion to help navigate pressing questions or concerns. **Sixteen percent of young people reported turning to "no one" when feeling overwhelmed or unsure about something. Young people reported turning to "someone from [their] faith community" at the same low rate (16%).**

Nearly 1 in 5 young people (18%) told Springtide they lost the practice of attending religious or spiritual services during the pandemic, and about the same percentage of respondents (20%) said they were happy that this connection was lost. Though nearly half of young people say they watched at least one religious or spiritual service online (44%), very few young people say they found joy (13%) or hope (14%) in these services. Just 12% say they hope virtual services continue after the pandemic.

A CLOSER LOOK
COVID-19

The uncertainty and instability brought on by the pandemic hit many young people hard. It was not just a road bump on an otherwise mapped-out route, but an abrupt detour that upended their expectations and plans.

Many young people have missed out on developmental markers and moments that are both formative and singular; once missed, they're gone.

> **57%** of young people ages 13 to 25 told us, **"When the pandemic is over, I expect a lot will be different, in mostly disappointing ways."**

Read about these findings in our Social Distance Study.

springtideresearch.org /the-state-2021-resources

READ

COVID-19

In April 2020, as the spread of COVID-19 was causing increasing disruption in the United States, Springtide conducted research that demonstrated, even early on, the difficulties young people faced due to social distancing and sheltering in place.

Nearly a year later, in February 2021, and nearly a year into living with varying degrees of restriction, Springtide spoke with and surveyed young people again, this time about living in and emerging from the pandemic.

Prisha, a young Hindu woman Springtide interviewed for this report, describes how life amid the pandemic was difficult at first, full of fear and uncertainty, but she also related how she slowly adjusted to the demands of lockdown.

> I gradually took small steps. When I was at my lowest point, I wouldn't shower every day. So I started by making an effort to get up and shower, change my clothes, brush my hair, just take care of myself. It took some building up, almost like exposure therapy, because initially I was afraid of even being near people, of bringing COVID back home. But just through exposure, facing these basic everyday tasks, I was able to feel more comfortable as time passed.
>
> —Prisha, 25

Prisha names how afraid she was. Many young people felt the same. And 74% of young people told us they hope to feel safe again when the pandemic is over. But fear of the virus was not the thing most young people told us was their biggest challenge.

The cost of the COVID-19 pandemic on relationships—with both people and institutions—was hard on young people.

A large proportion of young people (42%) say no one outside their home reached out to them to see if they were alright, leaving nearly half feeling isolated (47%) and without anyone to talk to about how they were feeling or what they were going through (47%). Though many young people spent lots of time at home around family members and roommates, 59% said that even while living with others, they still felt alone.

When you have felt overwhelmed and didn't know what to do about something, who did you turn to for help?

Participants were allowed to select more than one option.

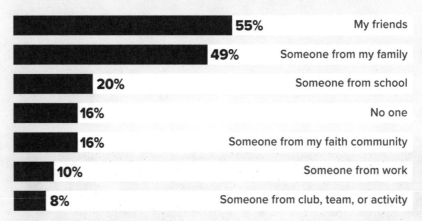

55%	My friends
49%	Someone from my family
20%	Someone from school
16%	No one
16%	Someone from my faith community
10%	Someone from work
8%	Someone from club, team, or activity

Nearly 70% of young people tell us that after the pandemic they "won't take for granted relationships and opportunities the way [they] did before."

COVID-19

A majority of young people (65%) didn't feel the government did its best to protect people during the pandemic. Young people had low confidence about feeling safe in church (18%) and spiritual gatherings (11%) during the pandemic. Over half (57%) of young people say it will take time to rebuild trust where it was lost.

Over half (57%)
of young people say **it will take time to rebuild trust where it was lost.**

Spaces where young people say they feel safe during the pandemic.
Participants were allowed to select more than one option.

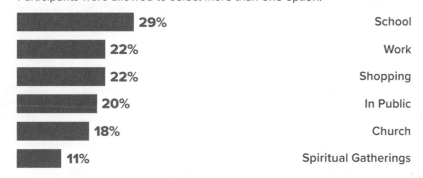

29%	School
22%	Work
22%	Shopping
20%	In Public
18%	Church
11%	Spiritual Gatherings

A CLOSER LOOK

Trusted guides can help young people make sense of their pandemic experiences and adjust to life after the pandemic. In *The New Normal: 8 Ways to Care for Gen Z in a Post-Pandemic World*, we offer eight research-informed ways that caring adults can help young people emerge from this season of upheaval and uncertainty.

1 **Create Safety** *to help young people regain their footing*

2 **Grieve What's Been Lost** *without dwelling on the negatives*

3 **Celebrate What's Been Gained** *without insisting on optimism*

4 **Resist Comparison** *by making space for a range of emotions*

5 **Get Together** *to combat isolation with intentional gatherings*

6 **Take Care of Your Body** *to help the body and mind process stress*

7 **Turn to the Arts** *to find new modes of expression*

8 **Focus on the Practical** *by offering young people concrete help*

The New Normal also offers exercises in empathy intended to equip trusted adults to guide young people as everyone emerges into a new normal. Download the guide for free at *springtideresearch.org/the-new-normal*.

COVID-19

The pandemic prompted Springtide's initial look at the way young people navigate uncertainly, and we've continued to explore this theme. We recognize that uncertainly is at the heart of adolescence and young adulthood, and also that responding to uncertainty is at the heart of many religions.

What does Springtide mean by *religious*?

For Springtide, the term *religious* is not a reference to a particular creed, code, or system, but rather a term that captures and categorizes a wide array of diverse impulses, questions, and connections. These are the impulses that inspire young people to pursue community, identity, meaning, and various practices. And we recognize that these impulses are increasingly finding expression in ways that may not seem overtly religious because they are not connected directly to a specific tradition or institution. Instead, the desire for meaning may show up in careers, club sports, or creative hobbies. Young people find outlets for justice, faith, or purpose in politics, volunteering, nature, and close relationships.

While we see the value in any activity that promotes the flourishing of young people, we also recognize the unique value traditional religion often can and does offer. From a sociological standpoint (as opposed to a theological one), we see the way religions, across creed and culture, can offer frames for living well, with careful consideration for congruence between the inner and outer life. We acknowledge the historical significance of religion for navigating times of uncertainty as well as questions of meaning, identity, and community, and it is from this starting point that we begin thinking about the ways young people are (or are not) engaging religion today.

At Springtide, we recognize the natural ways traditional religious institutions might be able to show up for young people in these seasons of upheaval. But we also know only 29% of young people who tell us they are actively part of a spiritual community also reached out to that community during a difficulty.

Why aren't young people turning to traditional religious rituals, practices, and communities when they navigate difficult or uncertain times?

Only 29%
of young people who tell us they are **actively part of a spiritual community also reached out to that community during a difficulty.**

The Disconnect

We wanted to find out why young people, even religious and spiritual young people, aren't turning to religion or traditional religious practices, beliefs, or communities when navigating difficulties. So we asked them: Why not?

Why, when facing uncertain and difficult times, do you not participate in religious practices or turn to religious communities?

Percentage of young people who agreed with each statement:

"I don't believe some of the things I hear talked about at religious gatherings."
60%

"I do not like to be told answers about faith and religion. I'd rather discover my own answers."
58%

"Because other things help me find meaning in my life, I don't need a faith community."
56%

"I don't feel like I can be my full self in a religious organization."
55%

"Religious communities try to fix my problem instead of just being there for me."
54%

"Religion, faith, or religious leaders will try to give me answers, but I am looking for something else."
53%

"Religious communities are rigid and restrictive, and that's not helpful to me."
52%

"I'm not sure how to get connected to a new faith community."

51%

"Because I have other communities, I don't need a faith community."

50%

"Religion is about certainty and doesn't welcome uncertainty, doubt, or asking questions."

49%

"Religious gatherings focus on topics that make me uncomfortable."

48%

"I don't think religion, faith, or religious leaders will care about the things I want to talk about or bring up during times of uncertainty."

47%

"I don't trust religion, faith, or religious leaders in those kinds of organizations."

47%

"I don't feel safe within religious or faith institutions."

45%

"I don't feel close enough to anyone that has a religion or faith to ask about it or share my thoughts."

43%

"I did not do anything with religion as a child."

42%

"I have been harmed by religion, faith, or a religious leader in the past."

39%

"I would not even think to go to a faith community because it is not something I've ever gone to before."

39%

A CLOSER LOOK

By no means is this list exhaustive, but it begins to demonstrate the complex and nuanced discernment behind young people's reluctance to seek out traditional religious responses when faced with uncertainty. While it is tempting to assume the reason for the disconnect is as simple as worship services are boring, in reality young people are taking seriously the weight of belief, the kind of response they receive when asking questions or expressing doubt, the example set by other people in the community, the difficulty of forging deep connections with a new community, and more.

More data can help unpack the list of reasons above.

51% of young people say they don't know how to get connected to a faith community even if they'd like to.

Religion is something to help manage stress and uncertainty. Well, I guess it hasn't really been that for me because I don't have, or I haven't found, a church that I like. But for my brother, religion has really helped him with everything. Like, he loves hearing that people have been praying for him and stuff, and it makes him feel a lot better. So I feel like religion definitely helps some people in tough times, but I just haven't found that yet.

—Jesse, 18

THE DISCONNECT

Only 14% of young people say they trust organized religion completely. Our 2020 report on Relational Authority shows a lack of integrity in relationships diminishes trust, and the same theme emerged in our 2021 interviews.

ALMOST
50% of young people tell us they don't turn to faith communities due to lack of trust in the people, beliefs, and systems of organized religion.

I think I'm farther away from a religious faith because I don't . . . I guess I just didn't like how my mom used it as a way to not take responsibility for her actions.

—Desiree, 22

Viola is a religious young woman who nonetheless recognizes the way religion can harm instead of help. With 39% telling us they've been harmed by religion, and 45% telling us they don't feel safe when it comes to religion, this is a significant experience among today's young people, even today's religious young people.

I have been exposed to people who've completely left the church because they've been hurt by it. And I've also visited some churches that I have really, really loved and resonated with, but I've also been really hurt by some, some churches as a whole, not just people and some of the basic beliefs that exclude other people or don't necessarily teach love. So I've had a really hard time with the Christian church, but I also really see the importance of having a congregation of people that all believe we originated from the same place and have the same love and spirituality.

—Viola, 17

39% of young people say they've been harmed by religion, and **45%** say they don't feel safe when it comes to religion. This is a significant experience among today's young people, even today's religious young people.

When it comes to shared values, half of young people don't think religious institutions care about the things that matter most to young people. We wanted to dig deeper into this observation, so we asked young people: How much do you care about this issue? And then we asked them how much they think religious communities with which they are familiar care about the same issue.

The Values Gap

Many young people don't think religious or faith communities care about the issues they care about.

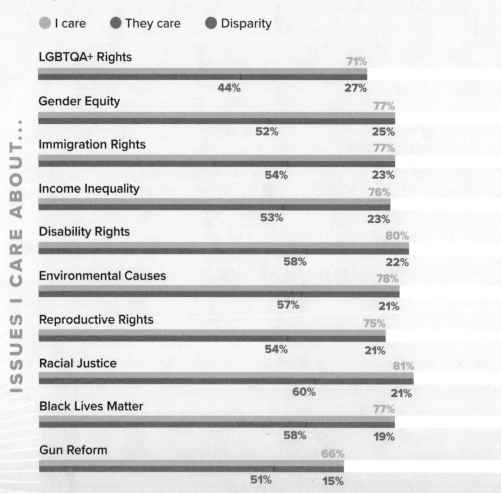

● I care ● They care ● Disparity

ISSUES I CARE ABOUT...

LGBTQA+ Rights
71%
44%   27%

Gender Equity
77%
52%   25%

Immigration Rights
77%
54%   23%

Income Inequality
76%
53%   23%

Disability Rights
80%
58%   22%

Environmental Causes
78%
57%   21%

Reproductive Rights
75%
54%   21%

Racial Justice
81%
60%   21%

Black Lives Matter
77%
58%   19%

Gun Reform
66%
51%   15%

THE DISCONNECT

Overall, atheists report the greatest percentage differential between their personal deep caring and their perception of how deeply faith communities care. That is, they care the most about these social concerns and are most likely to believe that religious institutions do not care much at all.

Almost 4 out of 5 young people expressed care for environmental causes, and more than half of young people tell us that going into nature is a religious experience for them. But there is a considerable disparity between how much they care about the environment and how much they perceive religious organizations care. The incongruence in values is stark.

For religious young people in particular, this sense of disconnect in shared values can be the issue that determines whether they will stay with a religious organization or not. Ethan is a young gay man raised in the Catholic Church and still wrestling with how and whether he can remain connected to it. More than any other issue, young people perceive a dramatic disconnect in values over the rights of LGBTQA+ people.

I'm gay. And I know that the conservative Christian community doesn't necessarily support people who are LGBTQ+. And a lot of the beliefs were written by members of the religion who don't necessarily respect these people. And so it's made me question to what extent can I really trust that this is what I should believe, that it is ethical or proper. And for that reason, I've kind of lost faith because I just feel like there's not a lot of trust I can place in the religion when there's a lot of hypocrisy and contradictions.

—Ethan, 21

Without a shared sense about what issues matter in the world, what precedent is there for believing that religious institutions will be a worthwhile guide in other areas of life?

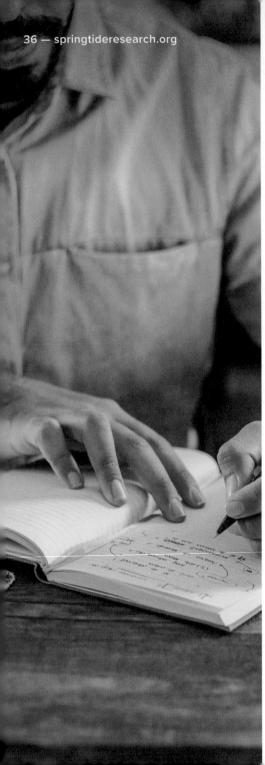

KEY FINDINGS

What Young People Are Telling Us

In 2021, we asked young people about particular crossroads that can evoke uncertainty: making decisions about the future; sudden events like death or disease; relationship transitions like breakups, divorce, or new partnerships; major events like graduating, moving, or starting a career. We asked the degree to which young people felt stressed, anxious, worried, confused, or scared when navigating uncertain circumstances, but we also asked whether they felt calm, confident, excited, or positive about whatever was coming next. We learned that young people are experiencing uncertainty right now.

40% say they **have experienced trauma**.

62% say they **have experienced emotional distress as a result of a challenging event.**

28% reported **experiencing a challenging event that was causing uncertainty or making them feel unsettled, uncomfortable, or stressed** at the time of completing the survey.

"Yes—I am experiencing this now"

- 25%
- 31%
- 32%

- ● Male-identifying
- ● Female-identifying
- ● Non-binary identifying

Through survey data gathered over the course of a year, nearly 1 in 3 young people told us they are CURRENTLY experiencing a challenging event. That means nearly 1 in every 3 young people in your life or care probably feels the same.

Despite this constant backdrop of uncertainty in young people's lived experience, a portrait of their resilience emerges.

> I feel like I'm a little more optimistic and positive than I would have been before because of experience that I've gone through already. I feel like there's nothing that can affect me as bad or, like, be as detrimental than what I've already experienced.
>
> —Lilly, 22

We know that the majority of young people consider themselves religious or spiritual. "Religious" can mean a range of things. It does not necessarily mean the whole package of religious beliefs, practices, or commitments to community.

> I'm not deeply religious, but I guess for me, religion is just something that kind of helps me when I'm feeling like I'm . . . like I need to believe in something. It can be calming, like when I pray.
>
> —Rene, 18

So we are not only interested in their experience of and responses to uncertainty but also in the role religion—the unique ways they are approaching beliefs, practices, identity, and community—plays as young people navigate uncertain times.

What You'll Find

On the following pages, we present a lot of data. We want you to emerge from our Key Findings with a sense of the big picture—large trends at work in the religious lives of young people as they navigate uncertainty.

KEY FINDINGS—ONE
Young People & Uncertainty

Young people are experiencing uncertainty right now about a range of events and realities they're facing. They are coping by turning to trusted relationships. By and large, those relationships don't include faith leaders.

KEY FINDINGS—TWO
Religious Identity & Uncertainty

A growing percentage of young people identify as "just Christian," a term that suggests a sense of being "religious" without being part of a particular tradition. Across the board, young people who tell us they are religious also tell us they are flourishing at higher rates in every aspect of their well-being and relationships.

KEY FINDINGS—THREE
Religious Beliefs & Uncertainty

What do religious and/or spiritual young people believe, exactly? We asked about a range of things: connection to nature, God, and others; doubt and trust in a higher power. More young people feel connected to nature than God. Twice as many young people believe in a higher power's existence than doubt it.

KEY FINDINGS—FOUR
Religious Practices & Uncertainty

Just as being religious doesn't necessarily mean believing certain things or identifying with a specific tradition, it also doesn't mean maintaining a prescribed set of practices. Young people turn to a variety of practices they deem religious.

KEY FINDINGS—FIVE
Relationships & Uncertainty

A fifth of young people say they aren't flourishing in their closest relationships, and many young people who identify as religious tell us they are not members of a religious community. But these types of relationships are the first place they think to turn in times of need—meaning 20% of young people don't necessarily have that help when facing life's biggest questions.

In Part II, we explore a concept called Faith Unbundled. Our data throughout Key Findings reveal that young people's religious identities are not necessarily tied to formal institutions' beliefs, practices, and communities. In other words, young people combine the elements of beliefs, practices, identity, and community from numerous sources, rather than from one, bundled-up tradition.

The following pages contain a lot of data. For more breakdowns of data based on race, gender, present religion, and region, go to
springtideresearch.org/the-state-2021-resources.

KEY FINDINGS—ONE

Young People & Uncertainty

Young people are experiencing uncertainty right now about a range of events and realities they're facing. They are coping by turning to trusted relationships. By and large, those relationships don't include faith leaders.

SPRINGTIDE™ NATIONAL RESEARCH RESULTS

© 2021 Springtide. Cite, share, and join the conversation at *springtideresearch.org.*

What's causing uncertainty?

What makes you feel unsettled, uncomfortable, or stressed?
Respondents could select more than one answer.

Making a decision that will affect my future
67%

Making a decision that can affect others
67%

Changes in relationships such as friendships, significant partnerships
65%

Changes in my life, such as school, job, home, etc.
64%

Not knowing what my life will be like next year
63%

Events such as disease, divorce, death, etc. in the lives of my loved ones
63%

Getting more responsibility
61%

Events such as disease, divorce, death, etc. in my life
60%

Relationships in general
60%

Getting older
55%

85% felt anxious about all of the options and choices that they had in front of them.

74% felt calm knowing they had the tools they needed to make a good decision.

What are young people looking for when trusted friends, mentors, guides, and relatives reach out in support?

What were the most useful or important things someone did to help during this challenging time?

Respondents could select more than one answer.

"Just let me talk to them"

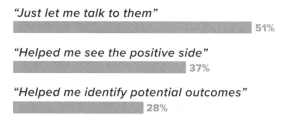

51%

"Helped me see the positive side"

37%

"Helped me identify potential outcomes"

28%

By a significant margin, young people found that a person being present and listening was the most helpful type of response they could receive from a friend, relative, or trusted adult in a time of challenge or difficulty.

Despite feeling uncertain, stressed, or anxious, they are confident they'll get through the difficulty.

85%
felt at least somewhat worried about making the wrong decision.

77%
felt confident because no matter what happened, they could get through it.

Ananya, a Sikh college student, captures this sense of both anxiety and confidence well, telling us in an interview,

> When I go to an event or meet someone I don't know, I feel very overwhelmed, but then, I've just got to remind myself that it's okay to feel overwhelmed. It's not a big deal and it will be okay.

—Ananya, 22

But how do they get through it? Where, to what, and to whom do they turn to cope?

Trusted relationships stand out as the top choice for young people who reach out for help during a difficult time. And despite the majority of young people telling us they are religious or spiritual, it's clear that faith leaders are not among those trusted bonds. Young people turned to "no one" in times of uncertainty as frequently as they turned to someone in their faith community.

Who did you turn to for help when you felt overwhelmed and didn't know what to do about something?

Respondents could select more than one answer.

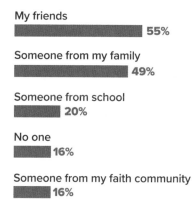

My friends
55%

Someone from my family
49%

Someone from school
20%

No one
16%

Someone from my faith community
16%

For more data on who young people turn to when coping with uncertainty, see graph on page 26.

KEY FINDINGS—TWO

Religious Identity & Uncertainty

A growing percentage of young people identify as "Just Christian," a term that suggests a sense of being "religious" without being part of a particular tradition. Across the board, young people who tell us they are religious also tell us they are flourishing at higher rates in every aspect of their well-being and relationships.

SPRINGTIDE™ NATIONAL RESEARCH RESULTS

© 2021 Springtide. Cite, share, and join the conversation at *springtideresearch.org.*

The Majority of Young People Consider Themselves Religious or Spiritual

What is your present religion?

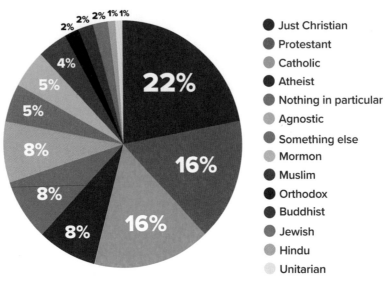

- Just Christian
- Protestant
- Catholic
- Atheist
- Nothing in particular
- Agnostic
- Something else
- Mormon
- Muslim
- Orthodox
- Buddhist
- Jewish
- Hindu
- Unitarian

A plurality of young people say their faith remained steady during the pandemic (47%). While 27% say they are doubting their faith more or lost their faith completely, nearly the same percentage (26%) say their faith has gotten stronger during the pandemic.

Percentages are approximate due to rounding.

The group identifying as "just Christian" suggests an emerging trend: many young people may be considering themselves religious but not part of a religious institution.

"

I'm not really into religion anymore. I just don't like it. Over the summer and last year, I built up a relationship with God. I don't like to attach any religion to it because I just don't have good experiences with things that are, that are said within Christianity and stuff like that. But after I build up, well, as I continue to build up a relationship with God, it's about just believing what God shared with me every day.

—Lauren, 18

Religious Young People Are Faring Better

Even without turning to religious practices or communities in times of uncertainty, young people who tell us they are religious are still faring better than their "not religious" counterparts.

The extent to which a young person says they are religious correlates with the extent to which they say they are flourishing. *This is true for every single indicator of well-being.*

Young people who tell us, "I am flourishing a lot . . ."

● Very Religious   ● Not Religious   ● Disparity

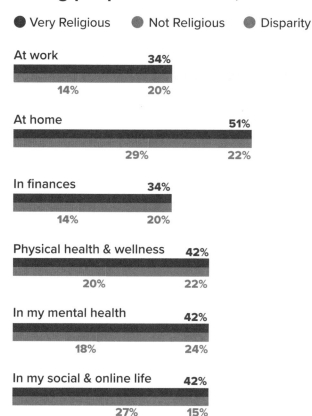

At work
34%
14%   20%

At home
51%
29%   22%

In finances
34%
14%   20%

Physical health & wellness
42%
20%   22%

In my mental health
42%
18%   24%

In my social & online life
42%
27%   15%

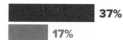

"I generally feel that what I do in my life is valuable and worthwhile."

● Very Religious   ● Not Religious

Strongly agree

37%

17%

Young people who are very religious are more than twice as likely to say they feel their life is valuable and worthwhile than those who are not religious at all.

Unlike levels of flourishing, young people who tell us they are "very religious" and those who tell us they are "not religious at all" experience similar levels of uncertainty: 55% (not religious) and 54% (very religious) tell us they have experienced uncertainty before.

While they may experience uncertainty at the same rates, they don't experience negative consequences associated with uncertainty the same. Of the young people who told us that they have experienced a challenging event in their lives that caused the feeling of being unsettled, uncomfortable, or stressed, only 14% say they are "very religious," compared to 30% who are "not religious at all." Simply put, this means that even though religious and nonreligious young people are experiencing uncertainty at the same rates, religious young people are not as negatively affected by it.

KEY FINDINGS

Young people identifying as religious but not necessarily identifying with a religious institution isn't just a Christian trend.

It's notable among young people of many religious backgrounds.

"Well, religion in general is a really complicated topic for me. Because, I mean, *yeah*, I'm Muslim. But then I feel I'm more like culturally Muslim because I don't really believe in any sort of "religion," I guess. I think a lot of people my age share my opinion about organized religions and churches and things like that— how harmful those can be. For older generations, it was like you *had* to be part of a church or some sort of organization in order to be a faithful kind of person. And I think my generation is kind of changing that narrative, and we can kind of believe whatever we want and still consider ourselves good people."

—Amira, 15

"[Faith] teaches you that no matter what happens, everything's gonna be okay, and faith itself can really pull you through. And it gives us something to look forward to, a destination. And I just feel like it's very, very important."

—Yadi, 20

Yadi affirms the importance of having faith in something. But what beliefs do young people hold in light of an unbundled approach to faith?

KEY FINDINGS—THREE

Religious Beliefs & Uncertainty

What do religious and/or spiritual young people believe, exactly? We asked about a range of things: connection to nature, God, and others; doubt and trust in a higher power. More young people feel connected to nature than God. Twice as many young people believe in a higher power's existence than doubt it.

SPRINGTIDE™ NATIONAL RESEARCH RESULTS

© 2021 Springtide. Cite, share, and join the conversation at *springtideresearch.org.*

The Majority of Young People Are Religious or Spiritual.
But what do they believe?

"Which statement comes closest to expressing what you believe about a higher power—whether it be God, gods, or some other divine source of universal energy?"

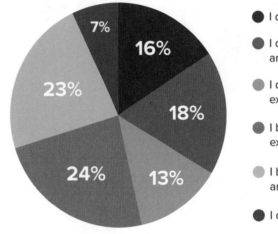

7% 16% 18% 13% 24% 23%

- I don't believe in a higher power.
- I don't know whether there is a higher power, and I don't believe there is any way to find out.
- I doubt a higher power's existence more than I believe.
- I believe in a higher power's existence more than I doubt.
- I believe a higher power exists, and I have no doubts about it.
- I don't know.

Percentages are approximate due to rounding.

I mostly went to see my friends, but I guess the faith aspect of these retreats was part of it. Like, struggling with the idea of even believing in God and knowing what or what not to believe. . . . That's something we talked about in these groups. It actually made me feel a little bit better. It's like, *oh, like we can have doubts.* We can struggle with these feelings and they're still, we're still valid, you know? So that was actually kind of refreshing.

—Milly, 25

For young people, believing a higher power may exist is *not* synonymous with feeling connected to that higher power.

To what extent do you feel connected to a higher power?

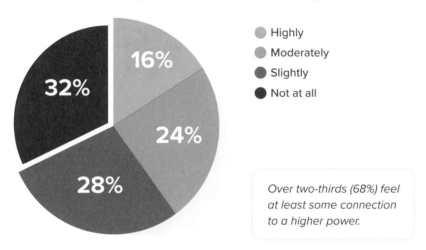

- Highly
- Moderately
- Slightly
- Not at all

16%
32%
24%
28%

> Over two-thirds (68%) feel at least some connection to a higher power.

Personally-held beliefs don't necessarily affect how young people go through the rest of life.

"I try hard to carry my religious beliefs over into all my other dealings in life."

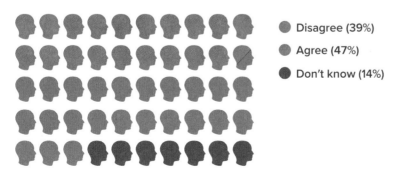

- Disagree (39%)
- Agree (47%)
- Don't know (14%)

Spiritual and religious young people don't *just* believe in a higher power. Among other things, an *unbundled faith* means young people don't turn only to traditional religious institutions for the elements of faith, but to several sources, including nature and relationships.

How connected do you feel to each of the following?

Young people who responded "moderately" or "high":

53%	Natural Environment
40%	Higher Power
39%	Humanity

A CLOSER LOOK

More young people feel connected to the natural environment than to all humanity or to a higher power. As reported in "A Closer Look: The Disconnect" (page 30), young people value caring for the environment, but they don't think religious institutions value it as much.

KEY FINDINGS—FOUR

Religious Practices & Uncertainty

Just as we know being religious doesn't necessarily mean believing certain things or identifying with a specific tradition, it also doesn't mean maintaining a prescribed set of practices. Young people turn to a variety of practices they deem religious, just as they turn to a variety of diverse practices when coping with uncertainty.

Identifying with a particular religion or spirituality doesn't automatically mean doing certain practices.

How often do you attend religious services (i.e., at a church, synagogue, mosque, temple, or other type of religious gathering place)?

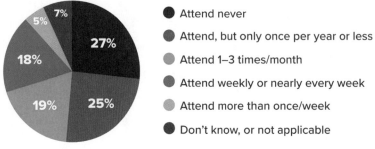

- Attend never
- Attend, but only once per year or less
- Attend 1–3 times/month
- Attend weekly or nearly every week
- Attend more than once/week
- Don't know, or not applicable

Percentages are approximate due to rounding.

How often do you engage in the following activity *as a spiritual or religious practice?*

● Weekly or more often ● Daily

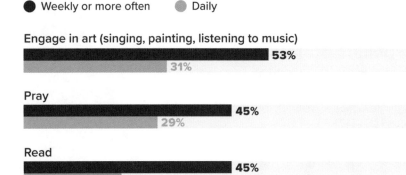

Engage in art (singing, painting, listening to music)
53%
31%

Pray
45%
29%

Read
45%
21%

Practice "being in nature"
45%
20%

Engage in yoga, martial arts, or other physical activity
40%
15%

I think I can still believe in God without having to go to church all the time. I don't think going to church is a bad thing, but I don't think it's like the end all be all.

—Carry, 15

For young people, religious and spiritual practices are not *just* attendance at explicitly religious or spiritual services.

How often do you engage in the following activity *as a spiritual or religious practice?* (Continued)

⚫ Weekly or more often　　⚪ Daily

Write
39%
18%

Meditate
29%
12%

Study a religious text
28%
12%

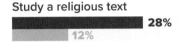

Do acts of service
29%
12%

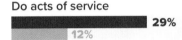

Attend religious or spiritual groups (not services)
25%
10%

For most activities, the category of respondents with the highest percentage are those who report more doubt than belief in a higher power. They may not be finding religious practices helpful within traditional institutional religion, but they are taking up religious practices at the highest rate.

> *Fewer than 1 in 4 young people selected "daily" or "weekly" for the handful of additional responses, which included making donations, fasting, honoring ancestors, reading tarot cards/ fortune-telling, teaching, and participating in acts of protest.*

My teacher introduced the class to something called mindfulness. And that is when you feel stressed and you take some time out of your day to just breathe in and out and not think about the past or the present, just focus on *the now* and the things that are around you that would help you release stress. So I tried that, and I really liked it. So if someone asked me to try, like, maybe yoga, I'd be open to it, to other kinds of practices. I joined one of the workshops, and I found it to be really fun. So yeah, I want to try things.

—Tyler, 18

Coping with Uncertainty

What were some of the things you did that helped you cope during your challenging or difficult time? ***Young people could select more than one answer.***

Talked to friends
44%

Did hobbies (baking, painting, sports, music, etc.)
39%

Played video games/watched shows or movies
38%

Talked to loved ones
36%

Talked to a trusted adult
33%

Prayed
29%

Stayed home and did nothing
28%

Took time in nature
24%

Connected with my faith community
19%

Worked more hours
18%

Went to a spiritual or religious gathering or service
13%

Read sacred text
13%

Helped others
10%

Connecting with a religious community (19%) was a more common way to cope in times of uncertainty than turning to a particular person from one's faith community (16%), which was reported on page 23.

KEY FINDINGS

Liliana, a college student, discusses how music is a religious practice for her.

"As a musician, even if I'm not actively involved in composing and singing or playing or anything like that, just *listening* to songs about God—or not even necessarily about God, but certain beautiful orchestral songs—they will hit me in a certain way. And I just feel God's presence, I guess. And I just feel way more connected with not only God but my surroundings. And it helps me ground myself more. And if I'm feeling sad, it will also calm me down and make me feel better."

—Liliana, 21

"Aside from a couple friends, I have my grandmother, who is very religious. I speak to her about it sometimes, but she has a very old-school mindset to where if I want to talk about a topic of LGBTQ+, it would be suppressed very easily and so on and so forth. I don't have a community. I . . . I know my university provides them, but also I've struggled with a bunch of classism in my university. So I kind of haven't been exposed to something like that."

—Christopher, 18

When facing uncertainty or difficulty, young people turn to close relationships more than anything else. Christopher explains who he feels he can turn to for various conversations.

KEY FINDINGS—FIVE

Relationships & Uncertainty

Many young people who identify as religious are not members of any religious communities. A fifth of young people say they aren't flourishing in their closest relationships, but these types of relationships are the first place they think to turn in times of need—meaning 20% of young people don't necessarily have that help when facing life's biggest questions.

SPRINGTIDE™ NATIONAL RESEARCH RESULTS

Flourishing or floundering in relationships

Almost 1 in 5 report *"not flourishing"* in relationships with friends and family.

3 in 10 report *"not flourishing"* in relationships with trusted adults.

Almost 1 in 5 report that they do *not* have someone in their life who really cares about them.

Many young people who identify with a religion are not members of a spiritual or religious community.

● "I am *not* a member/participant of a spiritual or religious community."

● "I am a member/participant of a spiritual or religious community."

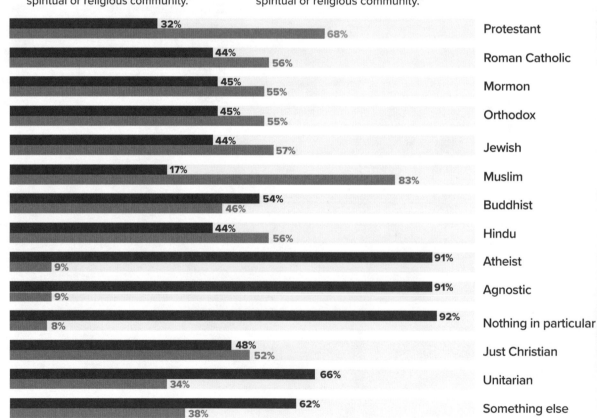

Religion	Not a member	A member
Protestant	32%	68%
Roman Catholic	44%	56%
Mormon	45%	55%
Orthodox	45%	55%
Jewish	44%	57%
Muslim	17%	83%
Buddhist	54%	46%
Hindu	44%	56%
Atheist	91%	9%
Agnostic	91%	9%
Nothing in particular	92%	8%
Just Christian	48%	52%
Unitarian	66%	34%
Something else	62%	38%

19% of those who say they are "very religious" say they are *not interested in being part of a faith community at all.*

Black or African American young people consider themselves committed to a religious or spiritual community at higher rates than any other young people.

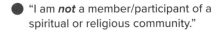 "I am **not** a member/participant of a spiritual or religious community."

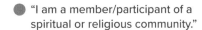 "I am a member/participant of a spiritual or religious community."

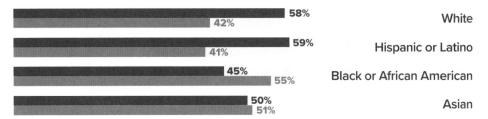

White — 58% / 42%

Hispanic or Latino — 59% / 41%

Black or African American — 45% / 55%

Asian — 50% / 51%

But young people across the board don't necessarily see community commitments affecting their beliefs.

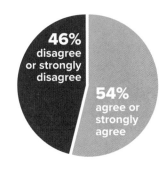

46% disagree or strongly disagree

54% agree or strongly agree

"I would not have the beliefs that I do without my community."

Even if they aren't embedded in religious communities, young people who are "very religious" report flourishing in their relationships at higher rates than those who say they are "not religious at all."

Of the young people who say they are *"flourishing a lot"* in . . .

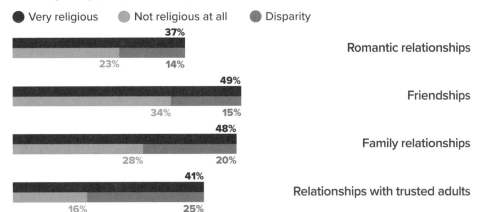

● Very religious ● Not religious at all ● Disparity

Romantic relationships — 37% / 23% / 14%

Friendships — 49% / 34% / 15%

Family relationships — 48% / 28% / 20%

Relationships with trusted adults — 41% / 16% / 25%

A CLOSER LOOK

Though those surveyed turn to close relationships, they don't reach out to faith leaders at very high rates. There are many reasons for this disconnect (see "A Closer Look: The Disconnect" on page 30), but looking at the times they do connect reveals what's needed to bridge that gap.

If you turn to a religious community, your faith, or a religious mentor when experiencing something uncertain, unknown, difficult, or new, why do you turn to them?

I feel comfortable with that community because I've been there since I was a child.
31%

I have friends there.
32%

I trust the leader of the community.
29%

They help me give back to the community.
21%

I don't turn to a religious community, my faith, or a religious mentor.
20%

(All other responses were selected by fewer than 20% of respondents.)

KEY FINDINGS

Takeaways & Insights

① Young People Are Uncertain

Almost 3 out of 10 young people report experiencing a challenging event that is causing uncertainty, discomfort, or stress in this moment. Twice as many young people turn to family (49%) and friends (55%) in times of need as they do to any other relationship. When they turn to that trusted person, the thing they want most, the thing that they say is most helpful, is the chance to just talk and be heard.

② They Aren't Turning To Religion

Young people said they turned to "no one" in a time of uncertainty as often as they turned to someone from a religious community (only 16%). This disconnect is a two-way street: young people report not reaching out to religious leaders in times of uncertainty and not being reached out to. Only 10% of young people heard from a faith leader or religious community during the COVID-19 pandemic.

③ But They Are Religious

Despite not turning to religious leaders, communities, practices, or beliefs in times of uncertainty or difficulty, the majority of young people identify as religious or spiritual. In other words, young people who identify as "religious" don't necessarily participate in religion in the traditional sense. The majority are not accepting the whole "bundle" of rituals, practices, and beliefs that religious institutions offer.

④ Those Who Are Religious Are Flourishing

Young people who identify as "religious" are more likely to report that they are flourishing in nearly every area of their health, well-being, and relationships. So whatever they're doing in this unbundled approach to faith seems to be working for their well-being.

> *This trend is worth a closer look by religious leaders caring for the inner and outer lives of young people.*

PART II
FAITH UNBUNDLED

What Is Faith Unbundled?

Our data are clear: young people are not turning to religious leaders, communities, practices, or beliefs in times of uncertainty or difficulty, though the majority of young people nonetheless identify as religious or spiritual.

In other words, young people who identify as "religious" don't necessarily participate in religion in the traditional sense. The majority are not accepting the whole "bundle" of rituals, practices, and beliefs that religious institutions offer.

Faith, or "being religious," among the youngest generations is more "unbundled" and worth a close look, especially because our data show that young people who identify as "religious" also report that in almost every facet of their lives they are flourishing more than young people who identify as "not religious."

So what is Faith Unbundled?

When we speak of faith in the report, we mean a person's beliefs about the self, others, nature, and the transcendent, along with the practices and rituals that express belief.

When we describe faith as unbundled, we mean that religious young people are not relying on a single religious tradition or organization to form and inform their beliefs and practices. Instead, they mix together things from various traditions, religious and otherwise.

> *Faith Unbundled* is a term that describes the way young people increasingly construct their faith by combining elements such as beliefs, identity, practices, and community from a variety of religious and non-religious sources, rather than receiving all these things from a single, intact system or tradition.

An analogy may help to illustrate Faith Unbundled. Think of how music streaming services like Pandora or Spotify unbundle albums: a person can enjoy specific tracks without buying the whole album. Someone can create their own playlists by "unbundling" a variety of albums and "bundling" songs from these many albums and artists to their liking rather than the musician's original grouping. In essence, young people with unbundled faith will partake in religion, including practices, beliefs, and communities, to the degree that suits them, with no formal or permanent commitment.

7

Watch Dr. Josh Packard talk with Crystal Chiang and Brett Ryan Talley about youth ministry and Gen Z.

springtideresearch.org /the-state-2021-resources

Read, in our Voices of Young People blog, about how seven student filmmakers turned to art to process the pandemic.

springtideresearch.org /the-state-2021-resources

More than half of young people **(53%)** say, **"I agree with some, but not all, of the things my religion teaches,"** and, **"I don't feel like I need to be connected to a specific religion" (55%).**

Nearly half of young people **(47%)** say, **"I feel like I could fit in with many different religions."**

To make this analogy more accurate, however, we'd have to imagine a way to add nonmusical tracks to this personally constructed playlist. Young people aren't *just* turning to religious institutions to construct the elements of faith. Our data show that they are turning to nature, pets, music, friends, and more.

The top five most meaningful activities that young people say bring fulfillment to their lives:

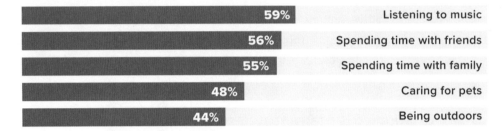

59%	Listening to music
56%	Spending time with friends
55%	Spending time with family
48%	Caring for pets
44%	Being outdoors

Because terms like *religious life, inner life,* and *spirituality* are commonly used interchangeably by those exploring faith, we use them similarly when talking about Faith Unbundled. This is an effort to better reflect the conversations happening among young people as well as practitioners and religious leaders.

Understanding the Unbundling

Springtide sees the phenomenon of Faith Unbundled expressed clearly in our data: young people who identify with a particular religion but adopt few or none of its practices; young people who attend religious services regularly but consider themselves agnostic, atheist, or nothing in particular; young people who are more than twice as likely to practice the arts as a "religious or spiritual practice" than attend weekly faith groups.

Young people are turning to a wide range of traditions, practices, and beliefs when asking and answering important questions about their faith: What do I believe? Who am I? What is my purpose in the world? What practices have value?

Unbundling & the Role of Religion

The first observation of this trend toward the unbundling of religious practices, beliefs, identity, and communities arose in the work of scholars Angie Thurston, Casper ter Kuile, and Sue Phillips. In their report *Care of Souls*, the authors write, "Unbundling is the process of separating elements of value from a single collection of offerings." This unbundling is evidenced, they say, in the act of meaning-making: "Fifty years ago, most people in the United States relied on a single religious community to conduct spiritual practices, ritualize life moments, foster healing, connect to lineage, inspire morality, house transcendent experience, mark holidays, support family, serve the needy, work for justice, and—through art, song, text, and speech—tell and retell a common story to bind them together." Today, young people no longer rely on a single institution to make sense of their identity, engage a community, outline the boundaries of belief, or offer practices that mark significant life moments.

Others have noted this trend as well, including Ilia Delio, a religious sister and professor of theology. She captures some of this novel way of approaching questions of faith, spirituality, and religion in a 2018 article for Global Sisters Report: "The 21st-century religious seeker is not bound to a rigid paradigm of ideas but is just that, a seeker or a quester, one in search of meaning, community, identity, wholeness: essentially, God."

Delio writes, "The well-known phrase 'spiritual but not religious' captures this emerging [sense of faith,] where religion is not a closed system, but an open system that flows into and out of other systems such as science, ecology, socialization, and politics; that is, religion flows through relationships." Delio captures the way young people deliberately avoid closed systems of meaning in favor of something more "open," which is another way of describing "unbundled."

In addition to scholars like Thurston, ter Kuile, and Phillips, Catholic nuns like Delio, and sociological institutes like Springtide, His Holiness the Dalai Lama has written on this unbundling of meaning, community, and identity from organized religion.

In his book *Beyond Religion: Ethics for a Whole World*, the Dalai Lama acknowledges the social and cultural shifts that have an impact on the role religion can and does play in the lives of many, noting that "many people in the world no longer follow any particular religion," and that "as people of the world become ever more closely interconnected in an age of globalization and in multicultural societies, ethics based on any one religion would only appeal to some of us; it would not be meaningful for all."

Globalization and interconnection make sense of this unbundling trend. He goes on: "In the past, when peoples lived in relative isolation from one another—as we Tibetans lived quite happily for many centuries behind our wall of mountains—the fact that groups pursued their own religiously based approaches to ethics posed no difficulties." But today, because we don't live cut off from other systems of belief, we need "an approach to ethics which makes no recourse to religion and can be equally acceptable to those with faith and those without: a secular ethics."

UNBUNDLING & THE ROLE OF RELIGION

The Dalai Lama echoes what we see at work in the religious behaviors of young people. A question arises amid this data: How do religious leaders attend to the inner life of young people in their communities when most young people no longer depend exclusively on a common commitment to a single organized religion?

Springtide data allow us to dive deeper into the quality of this emerging norm and identify and define key hallmarks of Faith Unbundled. We invited practitioners who are already responding to this trend, from both within and outside of religious institutions, to offer some best practices for engaging with young people of unbundled faith.

The hallmarks of Faith Unbundled are Springtide's contribution to a wider conversation about the state of religion and young people in 2021.

The Hallmarks of Faith Unbundled

Faith Unbundled
describes the way young people increasingly construct their faith by combining elements such as beliefs, identity, practices, and community from a variety of religious and non religious sources rather than receiving all these things from a single, intact system or tradition.

Springtide wants to do more than just note the trend of unbundled faith among young people. We want to help religious and cultural leaders understand this unbundled faith so that they can better serve the needs of today's young people.

We are specifically interested in these spheres of beliefs, identity, practices, *and* community, *and* the religious or non-religious sources to which young people are turning to navigate within these spheres. As sociologists, we are watching behaviors. How does Faith Unbundled look in the lives of young people?

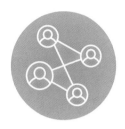

*What does it look like to unbundle **belief** from a single source or system?*

*What does it look like to unbundle **identity** from a single source or system?*

*What does it look like to unbundle **community** from a single source or system?*

*What does it look like to unbundle **practices** from a single source or system?*

We see the hallmarks of curiosity, wholeness, connection, and flexibility in our data and in our conversations with young people, practitioners, and experts.

It looks like young people who turn to many or various sources when making meaning and discerning what to believe about right and wrong, purpose and calling, salvation and suffering, and more. It looks like *curiosity*.

It looks like young people who are unwilling to shed parts of themselves to fit into a prescribed narrative about who and how to be in the world. It looks like a commitment to *wholeness*.

It looks like young people who show up where trusted personal relationships exist or new ones seem possible, young people who are willing to forgo participation in communities lacking these qualities, even if they have had long-term associations with these communities. It looks like *connection*.

It looks like young people who blend and adapt various rituals and behaviors to suit and make sense of the current questions they're facing. It looks like *flexibility*.

In this part of the report, we share the reflections of four practitioners and experts on how they encourage the flourishing of young people in light of—not in spite of—this unbundled approach to the questions and concerns of their faith. From their insights, we draw practical tips in conversation with our qualitative and quantitative data.

Watch Dr. Josh Packard interview Harrison Blum and Rev. Sumi Kim on what attracts Gen Z to Buddhism.

springtideresearch.org /the-state-2021-resources

BELIEFS UNBUNDLED
Curiosity Is the Vehicle

Insights from Rev. Sumi Loundon Kim

As a university chaplain, students usually come to me with one of four major issues: matters of stress, suffering, salvation, and existential questions. While on the one hand they're seeking concrete answers and a feeling of certainty about who they are, where they're going, and the meaning of life, they're driven by intense curiosity and an openness to learning beyond what they currently know.

My response to the curiosity that I witness in young adults depends on who walks through my door. I would say that there are three types of seekers, and each merits a different type of guidance.

First, there are young people who are completely unchurched. "Unchurched" is probably too generous of a characterization because "church" or anything like it isn't even in their vocabulary or map of the world. These individuals often don't know the difference between the words *atheist* and *agnostic*, nor know anything about religion or even spirituality. But they are searching for *something*, and they have a sense that there's more to life than education, family, and work. My response is to offer them some basic orientation and skills in beginning a spiritual path. *Here's how to sit still and listen to that small, inner voice; here's what a religious text looks like; these are the reasons we need friendship and community.*

CURIOSITY

If they have a religious heritage from their family of origin—which might need to be traced to grandparents or earlier—I invite them to learn more about that, as well. In essence, they need a starting point, and I try to help them find one.

Second, there are young people who were raised in a particular tradition but are starting to question or move away from it. Perhaps the faith of their childhood was presented with simpler ideas and they are starting to find those don't work when facing the complexities of adulthood or the uncertainties that the past year posed. I often affirm the richness and depth of what they were raised with, because they can get very disillusioned with their home faith traditions. But I suggest two things. First, I suggest that they may need to relearn their tradition's teachings with the adult mind they now have. And second, I encourage them to explore other religions, including Buddhism. For those who've come from a stricter or narrower background, sometimes that permission to explore is revelatory. Churched students also tend to assume that in attending a Buddhist group, they'll need to convert or "subscribe" to the whole thing. I say, no, just explore, come for meditation, learn about the Buddhist perspective, and if it works for you, then keep coming. No expectations on attendance or commitment; we hold this lightly and loosely. This type of young adult is often surprised that I'm not trying to recruit them and that someone from outside their religion sees its value.

Third, I see young people walk through my door who are in a process that is between an unchurched person just starting to figure out a spiritual path and a heavily churched person who's clearly rejecting their childhood faith tradition and thinking Buddhism is a good, new possibility for them. They may have been raised with a tradition that they've already started to move away from or question, or they may have had some exposure to religion through occasional participation in church as a child but not feel strongly influenced or identified with it. They may identify as atheist or agnostic. Often these young people are serious with their questions and have started reading books or taking philosophy courses. Their questions are astute and sharp, and their curiosity is intense and pointed. My response to these young people is to help them broaden beyond philosophical or intellectual inquiry to show that a spiritual path is also comprised of practices, community, service, emotional health, rituals, and so on. I try to point their intellectual curiosity toward including these other facets of a spiritual life, and to balance the headspace with a heartspace so that both are involved in answering their questions.

For all three of these types, what they often don't know they're missing (yet so desperately need) is a community where they feel like they belong. In these young adult years, the need to belong to a group is intense because that chosen group serves as a transition from the family of origin to the wider world.

In that regard, the Buddhist community in a university serves as a space for belonging, allowing different types of young seekers driven by curiosity to be with each other.

Rev. Sumi Loundon Kim

Rev. Sumi Loundon Kim is the Buddhist chaplain at Yale University and served in the same capacity at Duke University. She is the author of Blue Jean Buddha: Voices of Young Buddhists *and its sequel* The Buddha's Apprentices, *among other books.*

Rebundling Belief through Curiosity

A core reality of this unbundling approach to faith is not feeling bound to a single institution, system, or tradition. Fifty-eight percent of young people tell us, "I do not like to be told answers about faith and religions, I'd rather discover my own answers." Eighty-two percent of young people say they love learning new things. Sam's curiosity about contemplative practices opened a door to exploring several religious traditions:

58% of young people tell us, **"I do not like to be told answers about faith and religions, I'd rather discover my own answers."**

82% of young people say they love learning new things.

I regularly practice centering prayer and was involved in a centering prayer group, which wasn't technically Catholic, but just kind of general. But through that, I discovered a lot of other kinds of inner spiritual traditions. I like to say, when you're finding God in silence, it doesn't really matter what you call God: it's the same God. The Sufi tradition in Islam, I find, resonates with my experiences. Also, the contemplative tradition and different Indian practices of non-duality and mindfulness, Buddhism, all these things.

—Sam, 18

CURIOSITY

A reason behind this trend is that Gen Z has not necessarily "inherited" one single, coherent religious or spiritual system from their parents or mentors. When asked about reasons for turning (or not) to a religion in times of uncertainty, 42% of young people told us, "I did not do anything with religion as a child," and 39% said, "I would not even think to go to a faith community because it is not something I've ever gone to before." But young Americans are not simply "unchurched" or "unmosqued." They are, as Rev. Sumi notes, religiously illiterate, or naïve.

Young people raised without a faith tradition don't feel tension when looking to many sources for meaning. Whether turning to the rituals of various religious traditions, the advice of good friends, the subtle bloom of spring flowers, the *aha*'s that emerge from self-reflection, or the perspective that comes from praying to a higher power or reading sacred texts, young people whose faith is unbundled are not guided so much by an institution as by their personal sense of curiosity.

Tide-Turning Tip

Realize that curiosity is the vehicle for young people to work out what they believe about suffering, stress, salvation, existence, and more. We know from our data that they will turn to trusted relationships when they have questions or concerns about how to live a meaningful life or navigate an uncertain time. Rev. Sumi builds these relationships of trust by noticing where their curiosity has taken them in their religious question-asking: Are they just beginning to face some of life's biggest questions? Are they already sharply curious? Do they need permission to explore without recruitment, or a conversation about the goals of such curious seeking?

Curiosity is a driving characteristic of this emerging kind of faith that may transcend traditional boundaries. Some of the great mystics, prophets, and founders of religions also transcended the prescribed boundaries of their traditions at the time. Young people may be curious about the traditions that have shaped your beliefs and practices; when you share, you provide for and expand their religious literacy. Look for what you can harness in the wisdom of your tradition to encourage curiosity that drives young people's religious question-asking.

Wholeness in Well-Being

Insights from Nima Dahir

The process of the unbundling is something I resonate with. It makes natural sense to me when I think of my generation, as a Millennial, and the generations younger than me. Young people are reconsidering what to take as a "given" in their faith journeys. There is often a negative connotation of picking and choosing, certain judgments made about how these religious questions are held or pursued. But what young people are exhibiting with unbundling is not picking and choosing for ease; it's not a refusal to sacrifice. No. These are individualized, thoughtful decisions rooted in a commitment to personal well-being and flourishing. Young people are searching for a faith practice that resonates with them and gives them a sense of attachment to, and belonging within, the community.

Well-being is really at the heart of this desire for wholeness: young people have the language to talk about their physical, spiritual, mental, emotional, relational, and psychological well-being. They are leading the conversations around a more holistic view of what it means to be healthy. And when it comes to religious commitments, young people today are less willing to sacrifice one type of well-being for another type of well-being. They won't take the trade-off. Real wholeness wouldn't require a trade-off: getting to flourish spiritually but at the cost of your relationships, getting to flourish physically but at the cost of mental wellness, etc. Wholeness means the whole picture, well-being in the whole person.

I work with and study immigrant populations, and there's an interesting nuance to mention about this overall trend toward wholeness. In many instances, the "whole package"—the box containing everything it means to be Muslim, for instance—is important. People find comfort, security, and certainty in having bundled-up clarity:

WHOLENESS

"This is who we are, this is what we do!" The religion confers something rigid, but that rigidity is often welcome. It makes it easier to move safely through a new world, because some of the guesswork is gone. It helps give concrete footing in contrast to the fluctuating circumstances. I can see why this is valuable for some populations, including why it was important for many generations before.

If a young person came to me with this guiding desire for wholeness as they took up religious questions, I would affirm this value right away. I would tell this young person that the quest for wholeness is a meaningful inroad to faith and spirituality and encourage them to use the mindfulness that spirituality grants us to specify and identify their own sense of self and how faith can serve them in the quest to be their best selves. Finally, I would remind them that seeking wholeness (and seeking all well-being) is both individual *and* communal and encourage them to lean on loved ones and other communities in their development of self and in their search for wholeness.

Religious traditions have long offered a type of wholeness to individuals: here is a comprehensive way to live, to believe, and to practice the good life, the whole picture, all bundled up.

Nima Dahir
Nima Dahir, from Columbus, Ohio, is a PhD candidate in sociology at Stanford University, where her work focuses on neighborhood change and immigration.

Rebundling Identity through Wholeness

Young people today seek wholeness. Specifically, they want to experience wholeness in their life. They want to feel that their whole self is welcomed and even celebrated within a group or organization, rather than feel they need to change, fix, or hide parts of themselves. This doesn't mean they aren't interested in growth (85% tell us, "I believe in personal growth") but that integrity and authenticity are more valuable to them than conformity. In fact, the vast majority say "being authentic" is an all-important value for them (84%).

85% of young people believe in personal growth.

84% say being authentic is an all-important value.

It's no surprise they have little tolerance for spaces that encourage shedding or hiding parts of the self. Ethan, who is gay, discusses this kind of decision-making in his choice to remain Catholic:

> I'm just, I'm kind of in that gray area where, on one hand, I want to trust my religion just because that's what I've been raised with. But on the other hand, I know that parts of it just don't make sense to me. And I guess I'm going through life right now, trying to cherry-pick what makes sense to me and what I want to believe in.

—Ethan, 21

WHOLENESS

Fifty-five percent of young people say they don't turn to religion in times of distress because they don't feel they can be their "full self" in a religious organization. If their whole selves are not welcome, young people won't show up:

"I do not attend religious or spiritual services because I am not free to be who I am at religious gatherings or worship services."

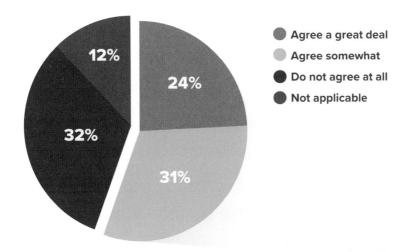

- Agree a great deal
- Agree somewhat
- Do not agree at all
- Not applicable

12%
24%
32%
31%

10

Watch Dr. Josh Packard and Tim Coons talk about belonging in an age of social isolation and disconnection.

springtideresearch.org /the-state-2021-resources

More than half of young people (55%) don't attend religious or spiritual services *because they don't feel free to be who they are at those kinds of gatherings.*

Gen Z is less interested in a complete and intact *system* and more interested in a complete and intact *self*, which may rely on and draw from many systems and traditions.

Tide-Turning Tip

Young people unwilling to deny parts of themselves that don't "fit" institutional norms will shed parts of that institution, if not the institution as a whole, rather than parts of themselves. But the shedding may not be readily apparent. Just as young people who tell us they are religious may not attend, believe, or practice their faith in ways that seem traditional, young people who still appear to fit into the box by outwardly practicing in conventional ways may be discerning whether they really belong.

If young people don't feel free to be themselves, they may find it difficult to fully explore the ways your religious tradition might help them become whole. Take time to assess your organization: does it send signals—subtle or otherwise—to young people that they are more valuable the more they conform to certain norms and the less they ask hard questions about religious beliefs and practices?

● ● ●

WHOLENESS

COMMUNITY UNBUNDLED

Collaborative Connections, Not Competitive Communities

Insights from Chris Stedman

When I was a humanist chaplain, I'd design programs just like typical religious programming. And I was often surprised at low attendance, especially when I'd meet a young person for coffee and find that their questions were the exact kind I was building a program to explore. I could have sunk more resources into better marketing, telling myself she would have come *if only she knew*. But I have since realized it wasn't an issue with the program's quality or the marketing or anything like that. It was the structure itself: opt-in programming when young people are already too busy. Sometimes the greatest gift I could give a young person was permission *not* to attend. But then I had to face the question of my role and work: How could I serve their needs if they didn't show up? What was this community without regular, well-attended gatherings?

I see a broad shift happening across many "givens": young people seem less and less inclined to tie their identity, their religious life, their political beliefs, and so on to any particular institution. And this can be a moment of clarity for institutions. Many dig their heels in and try to make superficial tweaks to their current programming to maintain appeal, but the issue isn't the programming. It isn't a problem with the instances of gathering, but with the institutions doing the gathering.

Here's what I mean: young people know they don't need to belong to a religious institution to benefit from religious ideas and practices. But I also see that belonging to an institution can make accessing those things *more* difficult, that it's *harder* to benefit

CONNECTION

from those ideas and practices while a part of that organization. Sometimes, the better, more effective way into a belief or practice is through smaller connections rather than overarching commitments, because the simple fact is that young people aren't likely to knock on the doors of a church or mosque and participate in religion in some wholesale way.

I think a lot of institutions (including those I belong to!) need to reimagine what belonging and participation looks like. If they are up for the challenge, the resources they have—things like institutional memory, rich practices, community rituals—will continue to serve the needs of young people. But if they won't reimagine the structure itself, young people will look elsewhere.

The reimagining has to do with how and where young people are already finding connection.

Religious institutions have to show up where young people already are: at protests and rallies, in higher ed seminars, at the workplace. Instead of competing with these other points of meaningful connection, share resources with them. Instead of asking young people to come *here* instead of *there*, meet them there. Join them at the places they are already making and finding life-giving connections, instead of demanding another block of time from their busy days or another commitment to a bundled-up community.

I eventually learned this when I transitioned from a chaplain to a professor. I have the chance to do the deep, thoughtful work with the students in my seminar that I rarely got to do with the ones in my care as a chaplain.

Why? Because they're already here.

The class I teach focuses on the search for meaning. I try to give students an opportunity to do what they're already doing in a piecemeal, DIY kind of way, the unique way they're constructing meaning outside of an institution.

CONNECTION

Because sometimes the work of constructing meaning piece by piece is slow, or reactive, or subconscious, as they respond to uncertainty or difficulty with whatever resources they have when it hits. My class gives them a chance to take stock of where they're at, where they're finding meaning in their life, and how they're navigating these questions.

I invite students to build a canon of meaningful texts that have helped shape who they are and their worldview. Then we look at those canons together: What's at work here? What do we find here? Often students have never before articulated what moves them or resonates. But initial articulations are footholds to deeper conversations about what matters to them, who they are, and who they are becoming. We spend time on spiritual and human questions in a place where they're already showing up.

Chris Stedman

Chris Stedman is the author of IRL: Finding Realness, Meaning, and Belonging in Our Digital Lives *(2020) and* Faitheist *(2012), writer and host of the narrative podcast* Unread *(2021), and has written for publications including* The Guardian, The Atlantic, BuzzFeed, Pitchfork, VICE, The LA Review of Books, *and* The Washington Post. *Previously the founding director of the Yale Humanist Community and a fellow at Yale University, Chris also served as a humanist chaplain at Harvard University and currently teaches in the department of religion and philosophy at Augsburg University in Minneapolis. To learn more, visit chrisstedmanwriter.com or follow him on Twitter, Instagram, or Facebook at @ChrisDStedman.*

11

Watch Aliza Kline talk with Dr. Josh Packard about how building Shabbat dinners helps young people feel connected.

springtideresearch.org /the-state-2021-resources

Rebundling Community through Connections

The hallmarks of Faith Unbundled relate to and build on each other. Young people are curious and will look to multiple sources to bundle the elements of their faith: their beliefs, identity, practices, and community. The unbundling of formal community membership—the kind that's tied directly to a traditional institution—means young people are instead participating in several, over-lapping communities, as long as those communities offer opportunities for genuine connection and do not diminish their sense of wholeness.

Springtide data consistently show that young people feel a sense of belonging when they have a *personal* connection within a community. Because young people don't join communities wholesale by signing up as members who believe, practice, and live in a prescribed way, they opt to define their commitments within a given community with a sense of nuance and even distance. That is, as Chris mentions above, they are reimaging participation:

> Sometimes I have found it really hard to identify with Christianity because of other Christians. And I know that's not necessarily right, because people are not always an accurate representation of the whole and of the belief, but I live in a really small town in a rural area and it can be really discouraging at times to have to identify with part of a church that I really disagree with at times. I don't currently attend a church, but I'll listen to sermons online and stuff. And I do some smaller Bible studies with friends.
>
> —Viola, 17

CONNECTION

Viola is uninterested in an overarching commitment to "a church that I really disagree with at times" but *is* interested in deep connections with friends on matters of faith. The local community of Christians isn't providing that, so she articulates a distance from that group while maintaining interpersonal relationships that meet her needs.

Just as Viola turns to friends rather than church for her faith connections, half of all young people ages 13 to 25 tell us, "I don't need a faith community, because I have other communities." Since only 7% of young people feel strongly that their spirituality is private, and 80% believe in trying to relate to others, these other communities, even if not explicitly related to their faith, may very well be meeting their spiritual and religious needs for connection.

 ## Tide-Turning Tip

Young people, as Chris notes, need help carving out intentional, guided space to ask and answer the questions of faith. For a variety of reasons, young people increasingly find that traditional religious organizations are not that space, though they continue to have the tools and rich resources to aid in the work of the inner life.

Instead of focusing on ways to bring young people into your community or through the doors of your organizations, think about ways you or your religious organization can partner with the spaces they're already in to offer resources for faith and help them forge meaningful connections with other people, not necessarily for the sake of eventual membership, but simply to support the religious flourishing of young people.

12

Read, in our Voices of Young People blog, about how participants in the Springtide Ambassadors Program define and experience community.

springtideresearch.org /the-state-2021-resources

FLEXIBILITY

Don't Fix the Flexibility

Insights from Rabbi Joshua Stanton

The majority of Jewish institutions in the United States came into being—at least in model, and very often in actual form—between 1880 and 1920, and they have more or less had the same goals since then. At the time, the institution's goal was to help a majority immigrant community settle into life in a new country. It has been a hundred years and more. Our community has integrated remarkably! And now we're just trying to sustain the institutions themselves. That has become the goal, instead of the means to the goal. I say this as the leader of a house of worship! That I love!

But religion needs to serve people's needs. And the simple reason that our religions are not drawing people is because they are not serving people's real needs. People feel compelled to join an institution to have their needs met. But, in the words of Rabbi Ben Spratt, "our purpose has petrified." And I suspect this is true of many religions.

Still, flexibility and fluidity is, or *can be*, at the heart of what it means to be Jewish. There are so many strands of belonging, so many *ways* to be Jewish. Why would we confine ourselves to just a couple notions of it? We are not a faith, per se, but a group of people with different strands in common (or *not in common*). And when you have enough in common, you get to join together in this wonderful heterogenous amalgamation called community.

The whole notion of sacred space, from the Tabernacle wandering around in the desert, was to hold space; to make space, and then allow for divine interactions to happen. Instead, religious leaders have been trained to take up space, to talk *at* people, to assume that they know they have more truth than they do. But what if we could just wonder together?

Young people are experiencing constant fluctuation, in internal and external ways. The circumstances of the past year, yes, but there are also people who experience fluidity in so many areas of their life. At a very human level, there are people who are going through the internal work of discovering a shift in their gender identity; there are people whose needs or interests or worldview is shifting and changing day by day. People are asking and answering religious questions in unique ways. And I see fluctuation constantly in young people because there is no one place that meets all their needs.

I see that part of my job is holding space so that they can deal with that flux in their religious and spiritual lives. My job is to help them see religion and spirituality through the lens of change. I hope to be a constant in their lives as the whole world is spinning around them. I want them to feel free, I want them to feel empowered in their spiritual journeys. I hope this gives them the chance to experience even more variation, to *lean into* the flux and the fluidity because they feel safe knowing they have a home base. Young people don't need me to fix the fluctuation, they need a consistent presence as they work to navigate it.

So when a young person is holding on to the value of flexibility as they navigate religious and spiritual questions, I respond in a simple way. I ask for their story. Because their story is what connects the dots. And until I understand how their practices connect to their lived experiences, I won't understand the internal logic that brings together a life of meaning for them.

Photo is courtesy of Hannah Stampleman

Rabbi Joshua Stanton

Rabbi Joshua Stanton is spiritual Co-leader of East End Temple and Senior Fellow at CLAL — The National Jewish Center for Learning and Leadership. His interviews and writings have appeared in a dozen languages, and he is currently working on a book with Rabbi Benjamin Spratt, whose ideas are interwoven in this section. You can find him on Twitter @JoshuaMZStanton.

Rebundling Practices through Flexibility

More than half of young people (52%) tell us, "Religious communities are rigid, restrictive, and that's not helpful to me." Young people aren't looking for static answers to dynamic questions. They don't expect simple solutions to complex bouts of uncertainty, and they don't necessarily see religious institutions capable of the same nuance.

Unbundled faith is not defined by a static relationship to a system or institution. This makes the religiosity of young people inherently flexible. When systems of belief seem "closed" (to use Delio's term), they cut off the chance for curious exploration. In a phrase, it discourages religious and spiritual question-asking. In Alex's case, something more "open" is a requirement for any future involvement in religion:

I'm not doing anything in terms of spiritual life. I'm in this period where I need to like take a break from anything of that sort. I have a lot of feelings about some not-great experiences. So I'm working through that. But even in the future, I don't think my beliefs would change, but I think if someone invited me to something, I'd be like, sure. I'd be open to that. But only if I feel like it's like not going to be exclusionary and it's not really rigid. Only if it's pretty open. Then I think I'd be down.

—Alex, 18

FLEXIBILITY

Young people are inclined to build something from scratch from many sources rather than accept the precepts of a single institution.

 *Tide-Turning Tip*

Fifty-five percent of young people said the most helpful thing a person did for them while facing uncertainty was "just let [them] talk." Rabbi Joshua begins here, asking for the story that can connect the dots amid flexibility and fluidity in various parts of a person's life.

Listening well, especially about matters of community, meaning, identity, or faith, is an art form. It is not just about uncrossed arms or nodding along, but about witnessing a young person express something, possibly for the first time. Spend time actively practicing the art of listening by responding to someone's sharing with curiosity about—not advice for—who and how they are becoming.

• • •

Every new generation nuances the traditions they've inherited, whether those traditions are religious, spiritual, secular, or something else, to make sense and meaning of the particular circumstances of their lives. Gen Z, in that sense, is no different. But where they're similar in kind, they're different in degree: we know today's young people are less tied to religious institutions than were the generations before them. They are unique in how they're constructing their faith lives. The hallmarks of curiosity, wholeness, connection, and flexibility are the foundation of a new kind of faith, an unbundled faith, that adopts and adapts the parts of faith—beliefs, identity, community, and practices—from a range of traditions, religious or not. Karleigh, raised evangelical, puts it succinctly in an interview with Springtide. She says she is "not religious" and describes herself as "a more scientific person," thinking that God probably doesn't exist, but *might*. Still, she tells us, she is interested in finding "a way."

The different religions around the world are extremely fascinating. People who pray five times a day or who fast during the daytime are extremely dedicated. And I am amazed at what they do. Obviously not everyone wants to do this, but I just like to experience different religions. And then I can maybe at some point find a religion that I want to be part of. I probably won't find something I want to join. But even if people don't want to be part of a religion, just help young people find something—like a person, or an activity, or maybe not activity, but *a way*. So they connect and have faith in something that can support them and guide them in life.

—Karleigh, 16

When a young person's faith is unbundled from a single, intact religious system or tradition, often they lack guideposts or boundaries for discerning beliefs or practices. Leaders who make room for curiosity, wholeness, connection, and flexibility in the lives of young people can themselves become effective guideposts, the kind that young people can trust and turn to in times of uncertainty, or whenever they're facing life's biggest questions.

● ● ●

14

Read the blog post about the playlist that Springtide interns created by inviting young people to suggest songs that help express how they feel amid uncertainty.

springtideresearch.org /the-state-2021-resources

Conclusion

Uncertainty is at the heart of adolescence and young adulthood, with each year different from the last and looming questions about who and how to be in the world. For many young people, the past year intensified this already common experience of difficulty, change, and upheaval.

Uncertainty is also at the heart of many religious traditions. Perhaps more than any other modern institution, religion is unafraid of life's biggest questions.

The State of Religion & Young People 2021 investigates how young people experience and navigate these seasons of uncertainty. Who and what do they turn to when coping? What kind of help do they hope to receive when they turn to certain relationships or practices?

We learned that young people turn to family and friends in times of need more than twice as often as they turn to anyone else. And they turn to "no one" in times of uncertainty as often as they turn to someone from their faith community. This disconnect is a two-way street: young people report not reaching out to religious leaders in times of uncertainty, and not being reached out to.

But our data also reveal that despite not turning to religious leaders, communities, practices, or beliefs in times of uncertainty or difficulty, the majority of young people identify as "religious."

In other words, young people who identify as religious don't necessarily participate in religion in the traditional sense. The majority are not accepting the whole "bundle" of rituals, practices, and beliefs that religious institutions offer. They are approaching their faith differently.

Faith Unbundled describes the way young people increasingly construct their faith by combining elements such as beliefs, identity, practices, and community from a variety of religious and nonreligious sources rather than receiving all these things from a single, intact system or tradition.

Amid the trend toward this new, "unbundled" way of approaching faith, young people who identify as religious are more likely to report that they are flourishing in nearly every area of their health, well-being, and relationships.

When young people unbundle their beliefs, identity, community, and practices from a single religious system, their seeking will be marked by curiosity, wholeness, connection, and flexibility. Following the insights of four expert practitioners—Rev. Sumi, Nima, Chris, and Rabbi Joshua—leaders who make room for curiosity, wholeness, connection, and flexibility in the lives of young people can be the kind of guides young people trust and turn to in times of uncertainty, or whenever they're facing life's biggest questions.

Equipped with renewed understanding, critical insights, and expert advice, we hope this report helps you support the young people in your life even better, whether they are religious, spiritual, or secular, flourishing, floundering, or something in between.

Appendix
Research Methodology

Quantitative Research

Springtide Research Institute collects quantitative data through surveys and qualitative data through interviews. The quantitative data tell us what is happening. The qualitative data tell us why and how it is happening.

For the quantitative data in this report, we conducted five primary studies over the last year, beginning in the fall of 2020. While the specific phenomenon of each study varied, all projects contained a set of repeating, foundational questions to measure demographics, uncertainty, flourishing, and faith life. We surveyed a nationally representative sample of young people ages 13 to 25 in the United States, totaling 10,274 participants. The sample was weighted for age, gender, race, and region to match the demographics of the country and produces a margin of error of +/- 3%. The age, gender, racial, and regional demographics of this sample are as follows:

Age	Valid Percent
13 to 17	40%
18 to 25	60%
Total	100%

Gender	Valid Percent
Girl/Woman or Transgender Girl/Woman	51%
Boy/Man or Transgender Boy/Man	42%
Non-binary	7%
Total	100%

Race	Valid Percent
White	52%
Hispanic or Latino	18%
Black or African American	17%
American Indian or Alaska Native	1%
Asian	8%
Native Hawaiian / Pacific Islander	1%
Other	3%
Total	100%

Region	Valid Percent
Northeast	18%
Midwest	20%
South	39%
West	24%
Total	100%

Tables may not add up to exactly 100% due to rounding.

Qualitative Research

For the qualitative research, we conducted 65 in-depth interviews either in person, via telephone, or via video. Interviews focused on understanding how young people navigate uncertainty and dimensions of their faith lives. Conversations were guided but open-ended, allowing for as much direction as possible from the interviewee. Interviews were transcribed and then analyzed thematically.

Interviews and survey responses are confidential, and all names of research participants in this report are pseudonyms. For more information or to obtain the survey instrument or request access to the data sets, please contact us at *research@springtideresearch.org.*

Our questions about the dimensions of flourishing were inspired by the validated categories in the Netherlands Mental Health Survey and Incidence Study-2, as featured in an analysis of flourishing factors by Schotanus-Dijkstra et al. (2015). To construct our flourishing scale, the dimensions were combined in a similar manner to the NEMESIS scale and used as an overall measure of flourishing.

Acknowledgments

Created by the publishing team of Springtide Research Institute.

Printed in the United States of America
5933
ISBN 978-1-64121-148-2

Research Team

Josh Packard, PhD, Executive Director

Megan Bissell, MA, Head of Research

Amanda Hernandez, MA, Associate Researcher

Adrianna Smell, MA, Associate Researcher

Sean Zimny, MA, Associate Researcher

Writing Team

Ellen Koneck, MAR, Head of Writing & Editing

Josh Packard, PhD, Executive Director

Maura Thompson Hagarty, PhD, Developmental Editor

Lucy Cobble, Editorial Intern

Creative Design & Production Team

Steven Mino

Sigrid Lindholm

Becky Gochanour

Brooke Saron

Paul Peterson

References

Page 10—Markham Heid, "Science Explains Why Uncertainty Is So Hard on the Brain," *Elemental* (blog), *Medium*, March 19, 2020.

Page 28—Springtide Research Institute, *The New Normal: 8 Ways to Care for Gen Z in a Post-Pandemic World,* 2021.

Page 61—Angie Thurston, Casper ter Kuile, and Sue Phillips, *Care of Souls*, available on the website of Sacred Design Lab.

Pages 61–62—Ilia Delio, "Religious Life in the Future," Global Sisters Report (website), September 12, 2018.

Page 62—The Dalai Lama, "New Ethic for a Small Planet," *Lion's Roar*, July 17, 2017, adapted from The Dalai Lama, *Beyond Religion: Ethics for a Whole World*, New York: Houghton Mifflin Harcourt, 2011.

Photo Credits

(All photos appear on Unsplash unless otherwise indicated.)

Page 12—Emmanuel Ikwuegbu

Pages 18–19—Andrew Neel

Page 20—Etienne Boulanger

Page 25—Liam Martens

Page 36—Fa Barboza

Page 38—Soundtrap

Pages 56–57—Marcos Paulo Prado

Page 58—Priscilla Du Preez

Page 63—Ian Stauffer

Page 64—Mathilde Langevin

Page 71—Le Minh Phuong

Page 76—Joel Muniz

Page 83—Sung Wang

Page 85—AllGo

Page 86—Luke Porter

Resources Listed throughout the Report

The resources referenced in numbered marginal notes in this report, which are listed here, are available at springtideresearch.org/the-state-2021-resources.

RESOURCE 1

Page 5–Watch how members of our Springtide Ambassadors Program bring our Springtide Tribute to life with their creative interpretation and filmmaking skills.

RESOURCE 2

Page 14–Watch Dr. Josh Packard and Ryan Burge discuss the "nones" of religion, and young people who are growing into religion.

RESOURCE 3

Page 16–Watch Dr. Josh Packard explain why a sociological approach is needed to navigate religious identity among young people.

RESOURCE 4

Page 21–Watch some of Springtide's ambassadors discuss returning to campus in the fall and what the pandemic has meant for them.

RESOURCE 5

Page 23–Watch Dr. Josh Packard and Derrick Scott III talk about how non-white and queer young people are navigating church.

RESOURCE 6

Page 24–Read about these findings in our Social Distance Study.

RESOURCE 7

Page 59–Watch Dr. Josh Packard talk with Crystal Chiang and Brett Ryan Talley about youth ministry and Gen Z.

RESOURCE 8

Page 60–Read, in our Voices of Young People blog, about how seven student filmmakers turned to art to process the pandemic.

RESOURCE 9

Page 66–Watch Dr. Josh Packard interview Harrison Blum and Rev. Sumi Kim on what attracts Gen Z to Buddhism.

RESOURCE 10

Page 73–Watch Dr. Josh Packard and Tim Coons talk about belonging in an age of social isolation and disconnection.

RESOURCE 11

Page 77–Watch Aliza Kline talk with Dr. Josh Packard about how building Shabbat dinners helps young people feel connected.

RESOURCE 12

Page 79–Read, in our Voice of Young People blog, about how participants in the Springtide Ambassadors Program define and experience community.

RESOURCE 13

Page 80–Watch Dr. Josh Packard and Rabbi Joshua Stanton discuss how Jewish young people are navigating their spirituality.

RESOURCE 14

Page 85–Read the blog post about the playlist that Springtide interns created by inviting young people to suggest songs that help express how they feel amid uncertainty.

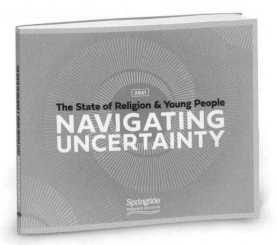

The free digital distribution of this report was made possible by a generous gift from an anonymous donor. We are deeply grateful for their partnership and support.

Are you interested in supporting future publications? Contact *giving@springtideresearch.org*

Support Springtide as we chart new paths for young people

- If you believe no young person should ever navigate life's most important questions alone, consider giving to our work.

- We equip people like you with new ways of caring for young people, rooted in research-based insights and bold actions.

- Support our work with a one-time gift, or by making a monthly tax-deductible gift.

As a 501-C3, Springtide will put every dollar toward studying shifting social, religious, and cultural landscapes, amplifying the voices of young people, and equipping the adults who care for them to care better.

springtideresearch.org/donations

Learn more so you can do more.

Move your organization forward, confidently. Our research services include program evaluation, grant support, custom surveys and data collection, and more. In addition, Dr. Josh Packard is available for presentations on Springtide data or the custom research you commission.

Contact Megan at *research@springtideresearch.org,* or visit *springtideresearch.org/services/custom-research* to learn more.

Program Evaluation

Grant Support

Custom Surveys & Research

Additional Custom Research Services

The Springtide Ambassadors Program

The Springtide Ambassadors Program (SAP) invites young people ages 13 to 23 to participate in cohort collaboration, personal reflection, and content contribution that directly impacts and influences Springtide's national research projects and publications.

Look for their experiences, expectations, insights, and perspectives as they shape and show up in our reports, website, podcasts, and elsewhere.

To learn more, visit *springtideresearch.org/sap*.